Angels, SATAN, and DEMONS

SWINDOLL
LEADERSHIP
LIBRARY

Angels,

Invisible
Beings
that Inhabit
the Spiritual
World

SATAN,
and
DEMONS

ROBERT LIGHTNER

CHARLES R. SWINDOLL, GENERAL EDITOR

WORD PUBLISHING
Nashville•London•Vancouver•Melbourne

402

ANGELS, SATAN, AND DEMONS
Swindoll Leadership Library

Published in association with Dallas Theological Seminary (DTS):
General Editor: Charles Swindoll
Managing Editor: Roy B. Zuck
The theological opinions expressed by the author are not necessarily the
official position of Dallas Theological Seminary.

Lightner, Robert Paul.
Angels, Satan & demons : invisible beings that inhabit the spiritual world / by
Robert Lightner.
p. cm.—(Swindoll leadership library)
Includes bibliographical references.
ISBN 0-8499-1371-3
1. Angels—Biblical teaching. 2. Devil—Biblical teaching.
3. Demonology—Biblical teaching. I. Title. II. Series.
BS680.A48L54   1998
235—dc21   98-26782
                                                                CIP

Printed in the United States of America
98 99 00 01 02 03 04 05 06 BVG 9 8 7 6 5 4 3 2 1

CONTENTS

Foreword   ix

Acknowledgments   xi

1   Today's Angels   1

2   Angels Yesterday and Today   9

3   Angels in the Bible   23

4   Angelic Activities in the Bible   37

5   The Angel Called God   55

6   The Angel Called Satan   65

7   Satan's Angels   85

    Excursus: The "Sons of God" in Genesis 6   94

    Excursus: The Spirits in Prison in 1 Peter 3   99

8   Satan, the Savior, and the Saints of God   105

9   God's Son and God's Angels   119

10 Demon Possession in the New Testament   129

11 Demon Exorcism in the New Testament   139

12 Spiritual Warfare—Man's Way and God's   151

13 Commonly Asked Questions about Angels and Demons   163

14 How Shall We Then Live?   179

    Endnotes   187

    Bibliography   197

    Scripture Index   199

    Subject Index   207

ILLUSTRATIONS

An Angel Declares the Resurrection of Christ   36

Angel Announces the Birth of John to Zacharias, The   xii

Annunciation, The   22

Balaam and the Angel of the Lord   54

Christ's Temptation   84

Elijah Nourished by an Angel   8

Jesus Casts Out Demons   138

Jesus Healing the Man Possessed with a Demon   128

Jesus' Agony in the Garden   118

Joseph Is Warned to Flee into Egypt   178

Peter Delivered from Prison   162

Satan, also called Lucifer   64

Saul Consults the Medium of Endor   150

Temptation of Jesus, The   104

To my wife, Pearl,

our daughters

Nancy, Nadine, and Natalie,

and their husbands

Dan, Carl, and Daniel,

with the prayer that they will

always resist the devil,

"standing firm in the faith"

(1 Pet. 5:9)

FOREWORD

———— ⬲ ————

I ENJOY LISTENING to Amy Grant's popular song "Angels Watching over Me." Very few Christian songs over the years have focused on angels as their primary theme. However, given the current fascination with angels, the spirit world, and all things supernatural, I'm not surprised Amy's song has done so well.

One of the more successful family programs currently airing on network TV is the weekly series *Touched by an Angel*. Each episode is a dramatic presentation of some mortal encountering an angel during a time of personal crisis and usually becoming a better person because of it. But many questions arise. Do angels come to the aid of anyone in need or just believers? Is the assistance of angels random, or are they dispatched from some central angelic location in the heavenlies? Can all unexplainable occurrences with the unknown world be attributed to *elect* angels?

These questions, along with the increasing fascination with the spirit realm, including demonic activity, make a volume such as this critical. In more than thirty years of pastoral ministry, I've observed few areas of theology that suffer from as much gross misunderstanding. If the church is confused on the subject, no wonder Hollywood can't be trusted to get it right!

That is why my longtime friend and colleague Dr. Robert Lightner has written a volume to clarify the Bible's teaching on angels, Satan, and demons. Because of his notable precision as a theologian and his broad experience as a pastor, teacher, and counselor, Lightner is able to penetrate the fog of popular myths and provide a calm, systematic overview of what the Bible has to say. He starts with the Scriptures and stays with the Scriptures, allowing the Bible to speak for itself. Following that thoroughly biblical analysis, Lightner adds his own wise and honest observations. What he has provided here is a convenient summary of the Bible's teaching on the subject that can be used as a handbook or study guide in various Bible study groups.

I know of few scholars today who are able to write with such conviction and authority on the subject of Satan, demonic activity, and spiritual warfare as Bob Lightner. Besides researching these themes in Scripture, he has experienced their reality during his many years serving as a pastor. He fully understands that these forces for good *and* evil described in Scripture are *very* real.

Now, as is often the case when studying lofty truths, the temptation for any author is to get caught up in the theological theories and lose sight of the practical implications. To keep this from occurring, Lightner wisely ends his study with a chapter title borrowed from the late Francis Schaeffer, "How Shall We Then Live?" Here he carefully offers practical suggestions on how to apply these truths and become more effective servants of our Lord.

This is a book you will treasure. Use it as a guide for a midweek series at your church. Share it with your small group. Take it on as a personal study.

—CHARLES R. SWINDOLL
General Editor

ACKNOWLEDGMENTS

I owe a debt of gratitude to Dr. Charles Swindoll for including me in this series and to the authors of dozens of sources used in the research for the work. Dr. Roy B. Zuck, managing editor, labored long, hard, and with expertise on this project. Thanks, Roy. My thanks, too, to Dr. Stanley Toussaint, consulting editor, for his valuable contribution. A very special word of thanks goes to my wife, Pearl, for her kind, painstaking persistence in helping make the book clear and reader-friendly as she labored at the computer preparing the manuscript for publication.

The Angel Announces the Birth of John to Zacharias
"And Zacharias was troubled when he saw him, and fear gripped him. But the angel
said to him, 'Do not be afraid, Zacharias, for your petition has been heard, and
your wife Elizabeth will bear you a son, and you will give him the name John'"
(Luke 1:12–13).

CHAPTER ONE
Today's Angels

ANGELS ARE APPEARING and disappearing everywhere these days. People with all kinds of religious orientation and some with none at all are reporting to the news media that angels have ministered to them. What are Bible-believing Christians to make of all this angel talk?

There was a time, not too long ago, when people outside the church and many inside it thought it silly and superstitious to believe angelic beings actually exist. That has changed. There is widespread belief that these spirit beings not only exist but also appear and minister to people.

Guideposts, for example, has recently begun publishing a bimonthly magazine, *Angels on Earth*. Every issue is filled with accounts of people who believe they have been touched by an angel or a group of angels. These stories are from and about ordinary people who have had extraordinary experiences they attribute to angelic contact.

ANGELS FOR SALE

Just about everywhere you turn you see little, winged, innocent-looking creatures representing angels. Recently a sheet full of "angel stamps to celebrate" came to my desk with the encouragement to say yes to the *Angels on Earth* magazine.

The April/May 1997 issue of the *Coin & Sportscards Wholesaler* carried an advertisement of a one-fifth-ounce gold gem "lucky angel" and a beautiful diamond-cut fourteen-karat gold bezel on a twenty-inch chain. Prospective buyers were told they could enjoy the power of the lucky angel. Beneath the advertisement was the fascinating story of the "Lucky Angels" history.

It began in 1793, when legend has it that the Angel's designer, Dupre, came close to losing his head on the guillotine. One stormy April morning poor Dupre found himself in a wagon heading toward the Place de la Concorde. At the guillotine the prisoners ascended the scaffold one by one. After more than a dozen men had gone to their death the sudden storm grew more intense. When it was Dupre's turn there was a huge flash and a bolt of lightning struck a nearby bell tower, causing people to scatter in all directions. The ceremony by the guillotine came to a sudden halt. Dupre was hauled back to the Bastille and was released five months later. Dupre told people that he was saved by a gold Angel in his pocket. It is said that Napoleon Bonaparte always carried a gold Angel. Historical legend records that he lost his Angel the day before his final defeat at Waterloo. By the mid-19th century the Angel's reputation was in full bloom. Officers, sea captains and businessmen kept a gold Angel on hand. In World War I, it is said that French pilots would rarely venture aloft without their lucky Angel. Hearing of this, a young German pilot by the name of Hermann Goering began carrying one. Some 20 years later, Goering became Hitler's Reichmarshall and head of the Luftwaffe. As such, he plundered occupied Europe for art and treasure. In particular, he sent agents out looking for French gold Angels. And they found thousands of them, most of which Goering kept for himself. But there was one group of people [to whom] he faithfully rewarded these French coins. That group was the Luftwaffe's fighter aces. Upon scoring his fifth kill, a pilot would receive his lady Angel from the Reichmarshall in person.[1]

Guideposts has recently introduced its Procession of Angels book series. The purchaser is told he or she can receive from the books "encounters with the divine." The first in the series is titled *All Night, All Day Angels Watching over Me*. Other titles to come include *Angels; Celebration of Angels; Angels around Us* and *There's an Angel on Your Shoulder; An Angel to*

Watch over Me and *What Children Tell Me about Angels; An Angel a Day* and *When Angels Appear.* Purchasing these books, it is promised, will open the door to angels in the buyer's life.

Few are probably aware that the parents of Nicole Brown Simpson and Marcia Clark, the prosecuting attorney, all wore angel jewelry at the O. J. Simpson trial. It is said they purchased the jewelry at a small store that features angels on practically all its products. The store was opened by the parents of a girl killed in an automobile accident. The girl had a fascination with angels, and just before her untimely death she said she would soon go to be with her angel. Her parents honored her unusual interest in angels by opening the store in her memory.[2]

ANGELS IMPERSONATED

Ordinary people are telling their stories about seeing and being helped by angels. These spirit beings are credited with finding and returning lost jewelry, healing people of incurable diseases, rescuing others from near-fatal accidents, and assisting in the rescue of the lost on land and sea. A recent issue of *People* magazine featured a cover story that reported several dramatic episodes of supposed encounters.[3]

Andy Lakey was an illegal drug user from age eleven. He claims to have had a vision on December 31, 1986. Before it came, at the age of twenty-seven, he was ringing in the New Year by freebasing cocaine in a friend's house in a suburb of San Diego. He became ill, so he went to his own apartment and got into the shower, hoping the cold water would revive him. He says he prayed for the first time since he was eight years old. In his prayer he promised God that if He would let him live, he would never do drugs again. Then he claims to have seen seven angels, who wrapped their arms around him. Then he became unconscious. When he awoke in the hospital, he felt totally free of drugs but never told anyone about seeing the angels until four years later. He began to draw them and soon quit his lucrative job and became a full-time artist. He admits, however, he did not know how to paint.

One day in 1993, Lakey claims, three robed and bearded men appeared before him, along with an extremely bright beam of light, while he was in his garage studio. These men said to Lakey, "We want you to paint two thousand angel paintings by the year 2000. We will give you the knowledge." After giving their message these angel-like creatures disappeared.

Soon he had finished six canvasses, three of which he displayed at a local bank. An art consultant was so impressed with Lakey's work that he suggested he do painting for the blind with three-dimensional paint application. It was not long until Peter Jennings bought and donated one of Lakey's paintings to New York City's Lighthouse Inn. Rumor has it that former President Reagan, talk-show hostess Oprah Winfrey, and other celebrities became fans of Lakey. He went public with his visions of angels and gives all the credit to the angels. Since 1993 he has completed almost two thousand angel paintings.[4]

COLLECTIBLE ANGELS

Here are just a few examples of how the marketplace has latched on to the angel craze.

Angels are collectibles these days. Of course, so are a lot of other things, like drinking glasses, cups, sewing thimbles, plates, and miniature houses, to name just a few. What is so unusual then about angels as collectibles? It is that only a short time ago very few people would have even thought of collecting souvenirs of angels. Many people thought only Bible-thumping, hellfire-and-brimstone-preaching fundamentalists believed in spirit beings. And who wanted to be associated with them? A glass-enclosed case full of angels would call for a lot of explaining.

All that has changed recently. Everybody, it seems, from the famous to the infamous believes in angels. Oprah Winfrey had a collection of 571 black angels. She recently donated them to the Angel Museum in Beloit, Wisconsin. Oprah's collection grew rapidly after she told Cher on one of her shows that black angels were hard to find. She then received so many from viewers that she had to tell them to please stop sending them.[5]

For your car you can buy a pewter guardian-angel visor clip for just $3.98. On the face of the angel clip appear these words: "Protect me, my passengers, and all who [sic] I pass by with a steady hand and a watchful eye." This is a prayer not to God but to an angel. Recently, Publishers

Clearing House offered an adorable teddy-babies angel figurine named "Glorious Glenda" free with a magazine subscription. For numismatics a keepsake coin angel is available. On it are the words, "May this angel watch over you, protect and guard your way." Nightshirts are available for women with a huge guardian angel in the center on the front. You can even write with a guardian-angel pen these days. On the pen is a fourteen-karat gold-plated angel. Cost: $4.95. Guardian-angel zipper pulls are also available. These easily attach to any zipper and add a "heavenly" touch. Angel magnets can be purchased to be placed on refrigerator doors. Four of them sell for $10.95. And thank-you cards with winged baby girls representing angels on them can be easily obtained.

Manufacturers and marketers know that since there is such a widespread interest in angels today, an angelic logo will sell just about anything. This is especially true if divine assistance is promised through it.

New Age enthusiasts have become heavily involved in angels. They draw on many sources for their beliefs. Several books they have written are especially important in knowing the New Age doctrine of angels and how it is at variance with much of what the Bible says about angels, Satan, and demons.[6] We will explore this in chapter 3.

"Angels in Fort Worth." This is the caption of two huge sculptured angels installed on the front of the new Nancy Lee and Perry R. Bass Performance Hall in Fort Worth, Texas. Each of the two sculptured angels is fifty feet tall and weighs eighty-seven tons. Each one holds a sixteen-foot-long gold leaf aluminum trumpet which extends over Fourth Street. The wings of the angels are more than twenty-five feet tall and span twenty feet. The two angels are anchored to a steel frame connected to the framework of the building. The head of each angel weighs about fifteen tons.[7] If this does not reflect current interest in angels, nothing does.

In his book *Angels and the New Spirituality* Duane Garrett has introduced two new terms to describe the unprecedented interest in angels these days. He describes this angel fever as "angelphilia" and those who are involved in it as "angelphiles."[8] These terms accurately describe the current angel craze and its advocates.

The rest of this book demonstrates that much of what is claimed about angels today is not paralleled in the Bible. That does not mean everything that is being reported today is imaginary or is of the devil. Angels are real. They are God's ministering spirits. The current "angel activity" today does afford us an opportunity to evaluate the claims, compare them with Scripture, and thereby benefit from the genuine and avoid the false and spectacular. To do this, of course, requires a knowledge of what the Bible says about angels, demons, and Satan. That is what this book is all about.

Elijah Nourished by an Angel
"And he lay down and slept under a juniper tree; and behold, there was an angel touching him, and he said to him, 'Arise, eat.'" (1 Kings 19:5)

CHAPTER TWO
Angels Yesterday and Today

—⌘—

OTALLY NEW GROUND is rarely broken in religion. Solomon's words are as true of religious ideas as they are of life in general: "That which has been is that which will be, and that which has been done is that which will be done. So, there is nothing new under the sun" (Eccles. 1:9). It is, therefore, wise for us to seek to understand what has been believed about angels, demons, and Satan in the history of the church.[1] Without it we will not be able to make much sense out of the current angel craze.[2]

THE ANCIENT PERIOD (A.D. 1–500)

There are indications that Christians have believed in the existence of good and evil angels from the very beginning of the Christian era. Angels, early believers said, were personal beings originally created by God in a state of perfection. Some of them rebelled against God and followed Satan in his rebellion. In the ancient period some held that angels had ethereal bodies—bodies of light. Later it was debated whether they had bodies at all.

The Roman world into which Christianity came was a society in which pagan polytheism and emperor worship were everywhere. These and other influences soon led some in the Christian community to worship angels. The archangel Michael was especially popular.

In this period of the church's history the fathers and apologists were occupied with the doctrines of God the Father, Christ, the Holy Spirit, man, sin, and salvation, and no concentrated effort was given to the study of angels.

The Gnostics of the second century did give some attention to angels, but their view had no scriptural basis. The term *Gnōstic* comes from the Greek *gnosis*, meaning knowledge. The Gnostics held that salvation was attained by acquiring special knowledge. Gnosticism, though held by some Jews, was a Gentile perversion of the gospel. It arose because of the widespread religious unrest and the desire to bring together all religious ideas and harmonize them. It was a syncretistic movement. Gnostics believed in two original principles, or gods, which were opposed to each other; their dualistic philosophy viewed spirit as good and matter as evil. The good god was spirit but was not identified with the God of the Bible. Opposing him was the demiurge, a subordinate god of matter who was identified as the God of the Old Testament. From the supreme good god there emanated a long chain of aeons—angelic beings—which constituted the divine essence and through which the highest god could relate to created beings. Christ was viewed as the first and highest of these aeons.

Important in the discussion of angels in the ancient period is the work of Dionysius the Areopagite, *Celestial Hierarchy*. Dionysius also wrote a series of short books claiming apostolic authority that had significant influence on the church. It is generally believed that Dionysius was a Syrian mystic who wrote about A.D. 500. He pretended to be the convert Paul referred to in Acts 17:34 as "Dionysius the Areopagite," who was a member of the Athenian council of elders (the Areopagus). Because of this pretension the Syrian mystic is accurately referred to as Pseudo-Dionysius.

The work of Pseudo-Dionysius is viewed as one of the greatest frauds in church history.[3] "Dionysius the Areopagite divided the angels into three classes: the first class consisting of Thrones, Cherubim, and Seraphim; the second, of Mights, Dominions, and Powers; and the third, of Principalities, archangels, and angels. The first class is represented as enjoying the closest communion with God; the second, as being enlightened by the first; and the third, as being enlightened by the second."[4]

John Calvin did not think very highly of Dionysius's work. The Reformer wrote, "If you read that book, you would think a man fallen from heaven recounted, not what he had learned, but what he had seen with his own eyes. Yet Paul, who had been caught up beyond the third heaven (2 Cor. 12:2), not only said nothing about it, but also testified that it is unlawful for any man to speak of the secret things that he has seen (12:4)."[5]

THE MIDDLE AGES (500–1500)

Compared with the ancient period, there was little sustained interest in angels on the scholarly level in the Middle Ages. Angels were believed to have been created at the same time as the material universe. The schoolmen, or scholastics as they were sometimes called, agreed that angels possess limited knowledge, given them at the time of their creation. Thomas Aquinas said angels could not gain new knowledge. Duns Scotus insisted to the contrary that they could acquire such knowledge through their own intellectual activity. In the Middle Ages the idea of guardian angels was viewed with favor.[6]

Without doubt, the greatest contribution to the study of angels in the medieval period was made by Thomas Aquinas, who provided for this period what Pseudo-Dionysius gave to the ancient era.

Aquinas (1224–74) is viewed by many as the greatest single influence on Christian thinking from the death of the apostles until the Protestant Reformation. He had much to say about angels, especially in his *Summa theologica*. Here he raised and in some cases gave extensive answers to 118 specific questions about angels.

Aquinas set forth eight proofs for the existence of angels. Just as the human soul exists apart from the body after death, so angels can and do exist without physical bodies, he argued.

Garrett's appraisal of Aquinas and his influence on our understanding of angels is valid.

> If we dismiss Aquinas as "prescientific" and therefore having nothing to say to us, however, we miss the insights of a man who profoundly wrestled with issues that confront us to the present day. For example, Thomas so formulated his doctrine of angels that he avoided entirely any kind of *monism*. This is the notion that "all is one" and it was near the center of heated academic

11

debates in his day;[7] in our day it has reappeared in a very different guise in the angelphilia of the New Age movement. As we shall see, monism has devastating consequences on our view of God (He is obliterated), ourselves (we become "God"), creation (it is illusory), and morality (it is insignficant). . . .

Aquinas also helped us understand the differences between God, ourselves, and the angels. Using a word you probably would not hear even on "Jeopardy," he said that angels are *aeviternal*. You and I and the physical world are *temporal*. We change both in ourselves (we can grow, go bald, or be burned to ashes) and in our actions (we can move to a different location or scratch our ears). God is *eternal*. This means more than that He exists forever; He is completely above time and change. Angels are *aeviternal*. They do not change in their nature but do change in their actions (they do not die or grow senile, but they do, for example, move from one place to another).[8]

THE REFORMATION (1500–1648)

Little new development in angelology can be found during the Reformation period. However, the Reformers did stress the reality of Satan and the demons of hell. While he was viewed as very wicked and powerful, it was emphasized that Satan could do only what God permitted him to do.

The attention given to holy angels in this period stressed their role in ministering to believers. Some believed strongly in guardian angels, and others denied their existence just as strongly. Article twelve of the Belgic Confession (1561) presents the generally accepted Calvinistic view of the time: "He also created the angels good, to be his messengers and to serve his elect: some of whom are fallen from that excellency, in which God created them, into everlasting perdition; and the others have, by the grace of God, remained steadfast and continued in their primitive state. The devils and evil spirits are so depraved that they are enemies of God and every good thing to the utmost of their power, as murderers watching to ruin the Church and every member thereof, and by their wicked stratagems to destroy all; and are therefore, by their own wickedness, adjudged to eternal damnation, daily expecting their horrible torments."[9]

Two outstanding contributions to angelology in this period came from John Calvin[10] and John Milton.

In keeping with all his writings, Calvin determined not to go beyond Scripture in what he said about angels. He believed the basics about good angels—they serve as God's ministering spirits for His own. Calvin did not enter into the discussions concerning the number and rank of angels. He was also hesitant to affirm the idea of a single guardian angel over each believer. He did believe though that holy angels as a group watch over the elect.

"Angels and devils play a major role in the great poetry of Western Civilization. In the *Divine Comedy*, Dante travels through hell, purgatory, and heaven in an allegorical pilgrimage of the soul. His Satan is remarkable for dwelling at the center of hell, not in sulfurous flames, but in a frozen lake. Goethe's *Faust* explores the depths of human experience with the dubious aid of Mephistopheles. Surely no epic of literature, however, focuses as totally on the realm of angels and demons as does John Milton's *Paradise Lost*."[11]

Milton's poem, *Paradise Lost*, dedicated to his daughters, has contributed most to the perception many have of angels and demons. The real question is whether *Paradise Lost* sets forth the Bible's message about these spirit beings.

It is a fact of history that Milton came to believe in an unorthodox view of God, though earlier in his life he had faithfully studied the Scriptures, especially the Old Testament. He believed Christ and the Holy Spirit were not as fully divine as God the Father. They were viewed as subordinate in essence to the Father. The Son, Milton believed, was a created being, which was what Arius the heretic also believed.

Some reject Milton's contribution to the subject of angels and demons in *Paradise Lost*, primarily because in it he subjects God the Father, Christ, angels, and even Satan to fantasizing. "Simply put, these very human spirits have little relation to the angels and demons of the Bible. As humans, we cannot tell a story that is anything other than a human story. In the very act of imagining spirits and inventing stories about them, we humanize them and so construct idols. These angels look less than angelic and these demons look better than demonic. We create spirits in our own image: this is the very essence of myth. As we are mixtures of good and evil, so are they. *Paradise Lost* is such a work; it is no more a story of real angels than Ovid's *Metamorphoses* is a story of real gods."[12]

THE MODERN PERIOD (1648–PRESENT)

The rationalism of the eighteenth century affected angelology just as it did all the other doctrines of the historic orthodox Christian faith. Along with the rejection of the Bible as the Word of God came the denial of the existence of angels. Liberal theology seeks to retain a semblance of belief in angels while viewing them simply as symbolic representations of God's care and concern.

Not too long ago those who believed in spirit beings were considered hopelessly naive. This is not so today, with the rise and invasion of the occult. Astrology, spiritism, witchcraft, and Satan worship are common and are growing in popularity all over the world. The book market has been flooded with publications by both occult sympathizers and those opposed to it. Evangelical publishing houses have marketed large numbers of titles that present the biblical doctrine of angels, demons, and Satan. Billy Graham's *Angels: God's Secret Agents* illustrates the interest in the subject. It sold over 750,000 copies quickly and was on the *New York Times* bestseller list for months. On the side of the occult is Ruth Montgomery's book *A Gift of Prophecy* about the so-called prophetess Jeanne Dixon. This sold over three million copies. Most daily newspapers in the United States carry astrology columns. Popular magazines continue to carry articles, sometimes including cover stories, dealing with Satan worship and demons.

Religion writer Louis Cassels was right when he called the upsurge of public interest in astrology, witchcraft, spiritualism, and other occult arts one of the most curious phenomena of American life. Of course, other parts of the world have experienced occult oppression for centuries. Why this resurgence of interest? Without doubt, the basic reason lies in the rejection of a totally inspired and authoritative Bible. When men turned away from God's Word, they turned to themselves for authority. Having experienced humanism's total failure and frustration, many people are now turning to the world of evil spirits for answers to their most perplexing problems. Another reason for the contemporary interest in and occasional practice of the occult may be that evangelical theology has said so little about the scriptural doctrines of angels, demons, and Satan. Into the vacuum created by this dearth of information have come subjective and unscriptural teachings.

In the modern period three individuals have made significant contributions to the study of angels.[13] Others are important, too, especially New Age enthusiasts, but these will be introduced later in this chapter.

Emanuel Swedenborg (1688–1772)

This man wrote over thirty books, claiming that angels guided him as he did so. He was a scientist who became a mystic. He said a vision from God changed his entire life, giving him insight into spiritual realms. After this life-changing experience, Swedenborg said, he talked freely with angels and they with him. The revelation he received through the vision was supposedly the realization of the predicted second coming of Christ. In his day he and his claims were not received by those who embraced historic Christianity. The fact that he denied the orthodox doctrine of the Trinity and held to a foreign doctrine of salvation also served to set him apart from orthodoxy.

"Many of Swedenborg's theories, with their combination of mysticism and eighteenth century science, are as peculiar as they are quaint. He taught that angels have many of the same characteristics as humans (eating, breathing, reading, enjoying marriage and sexuality, and so forth), and that godly people enjoy all these things after death too. Elsewhere, however, he conceived of angels as something like bubbles in the sky.... Also, apparently not content with the Genesis 1 version of things, Swedenborg taught that God did not create rats, scorpions, foxes, tigers, bats, crocodiles, frogs, snakes, owls, or the like. They come from hell."[14] When we summarize the New Age angelmania later in this chapter, we will see that some of Swedenborg's beliefs are still held today. Numbers of New Age writers set forth an angel-inspired religion, just as he did.

Karl Barth (1886–1968)

The father of what has come to be known as neoorthodox theology had much to say about angels. He insisted that all we believe about angels should be based solidly in the Bible. Because of this strong insistence Barth did not embrace much of what others before him, such as Pseudo-Dionysius and Thomas Aquinas, had believed and taught.

Barth also sought to relate all his angelology to Christ and His redemptive work. He did this even though his view of the Bible and his view of Christ were not in complete harmony with the historic orthodox position. Angels, Barth believed, are God's agents, but they cannot be known apart from knowing Him. Any human desire to make contact with angels is foolish, he said. Though real, angels have no reason to communicate with people. Angels bring heaven to earth, yet they always bear God's message, not their own. It is therefore idolatrous to worship them.

Barth contended that any view of angels that focuses on them and not on Christ is not in accord with the Bible.

Geddes MacGregor

As of this writing MacGregor is emeritus distinguished professor of philosophy at the University of Southern California. In his book *Angels: Ministers of Grace*, MacGregor advances the notion that angels are a super-race of evolved extraterrestrials.

MacGregor's view is based solidly on belief in evolution. He also believes that life exists on other planets, and that extraterrestrial spirits communicate with us as angels. Garrett points out that MacGregor's case fails for two reasons. "First, his scientific underpinnings are not as strong as he thinks. While this is not the place to go into it, the 'fact' of evolution, on which he builds his case, is not established. Notwithstanding the antiquity of the universe and the fossil record, the case for evolution has many shortcomings. . . . More to the point, however, is the fact that if what we call angels are really superevolved aliens, then they are not angels at all but are aliens pretending to be angels. An angel is not simply more powerful or more advanced than us but is altogether a different category of being."[15]

NEW AGE ANGELS

Before we can understand how New Agers view the spirit world, we need to know what the New Age religion is. Only the most basic tenets of New Ageism will be presented.

Tom Minnery defined this movement as "a hodgepodge of spirit worship, Hindu mysticism and avant-garde psychology. . . . Although the trend is called 'New Age,' its essence lies in ancient Hinduism which holds that everyone—and everything—is part of God, part of a divine 'oneness' within. Thus people need look no further than themselves for life's answers."[16]

Philip Lochhaas sees the New Age "movement" as "America's latest pop religion, a westernized and often commercialized form of Hinduism offering an olio of newfound love, prosperity and eternal happiness." Then he adds, "But it is far more than that. It is the most anti-God philosophy to come on the scene in recent years, a blatant repetition of Satan's first and most successful temptation: to be as God. Yet its various expressions have attracted students, laborers, housewives, clergymen and teachers, and a host of businessmen and captains of industry."[17]

Both of these definitions are accurate descriptions of the New Age phenomenon. Evangelicals view it as finding its roots in Hinduism, embracing pantheism—the belief that everyone and everything is part of God—and as vehemently opposed to biblical Christianity, either overtly or covertly.

New Age theology includes these eight points: (1) God and creation are one. God is an impersonal force or energy. (2) Revelation is special and continuous. The Bible is not authoritative. In fact, the four Gospels of the New Testament present symbolic details about the mysteries of God. (3) Humanity is one with God. Every person is divine. (4) Jesus is a man who evolved into a godlike being. The Christ spirit, an impersonal "force," dwelt in Jesus, just as it did in any number of other great religious leaders. (5) Humanity's crises are all the result of people's ignorance of their own divinity. (6) Humanity, therefore, needs a complete "transformation" in which each person is made aware of his or her oneness with God. (7) Through various techniques an altered state of consciousness can be produced in individuals, resulting in a perceived change of reality. (8) The "transformation" of each individual is the basis for the transformation of the entire world—"global transformation"—which will result in social unity.

In view of this background and these core beliefs, what do New Agers believe about angels?

Many books have been written on angels by New Agers. Here are several: Joan Webster Anderson, *Where Angels Walk;* Alma Daniel, Timothy Wyllie, and Andrew Ramer, *Ask Your Angels;* Sophy Burnham, *A Book of*

Angels; Terry Lynn Taylor, *Guardians of Hope*; Rosemary Ellen Guiley, *Angels of Mercy*; and John Randolph Price, *The Angels within Us*.

In these books and others like them the authors draw on various sources for their information. No distinction is made between the Koran, the Bible, the apocryphal New Testament books, the writings of Pseudo-Dionysius, or Swedenborg. The biblical angel Michael is not distinguished from the Mormon angel Moroni.

New Agers insist on knowing the names of their contact angels. This seems to give them a sense of security, authenticity, and reality to what they cannot always see. Much of New Age teaching, it is claimed, comes from angelic instruction. The angel Abigrael is acknowledged as the teacher for much of what is taught in *Ask Your Angels*.

Learning about angels from the New Age perspective can help a person self-actualize, we are told. This means escaping negatives and overcoming a poor self-image, thus realizing one's own divinity. New Age angelology combines Eastern mystical thinking and a popularized version of Western secular psychology, producing an incoherent and incomprehensible view of human nature. As Garrett explains, "On the psychological side, they believe that nothing is so destructive to human potential as guilt and fear. Their books all sing the same refrain: the only thing keeping you back from peace, joy, love, and complete self-actualization is the guilt and fear of your own ego. If you can escape these negatives, you will overcome the anger, frustration, and lack of purpose that confounds your every day. The quest for a healthy self-image ranks high on their agenda."[18]

The authors of *Ask Your Angels* describe angel activity as waves, and they suggest we are now in the "third wave." In Bible times, the time of the first wave, angels appeared only to a select few, such as the prophets and patriarchs. The second wave came in the Dark Ages or the medieval period. During this time angels appeared to outstanding Christians as well as significant leaders. At the present time, during the "third wave," angels reveal themselves to ordinary people.

Anyone can make contact and communicate with angels, we are told. Steps are given on how to access angels: Get rid of negative feelings from the past, be sure there are none still lingering, surrender the mind to the

"Spirit within," and meditate. After these steps are taken, a light will appear before you, which means you are approaching an angel. When the angel appears in physical form, and he or she will, you can ask for whatever you want. In this way you can reach your higher self.

Ask Your Angels tells the reader how to make direct angel contact. The exercise is called the G-R-A-C-E process. This stands for Grounding, Releasing, Aligning, Conversing, and Enjoying the angel contact. When conversation takes place between the person and the angel, a written record should be kept of the messages given by the angel.

Concentrated meditation on angels is also urged. This is especially beneficial when a bad thought enters one's mind. Visualizing an angel at such times serves to cleanse the mind. New Age enthusiasts draw freely on psychological techniques as means of ridding themselves of negative feelings. Angels become intermediaries to accomplish this.

It is said that angels also carry on activity with civilizations other than those of our own planet. A person's angel can tell him or her all about life on other planets.

When you are discouraged or depressed, angels can (and do) come to your rescue. They lift your spirits. New Age people are so deeply involved with spirit beings that they see them just about everywhere doing just about anything. There are angels for every occasion. Some are experts in one area of human need and others in another area.

Yes, the ancients did believe in angels. Some held more biblical views than others. Thomas Aquinas made significant contributions to the study of angels in the Middle Ages, while many others argued about how many angels could dance on the head of a pin. Calvin and Milton both made contributions, though not of equal value, to the study in the Reformation period.

Without doubt the modern period from 1648 to the present has witnessed more emphasis on angels, demons, and Satan than in any other period. By no means has it all been good. In New Age thinking, angels have replaced God, and for many the messages the angels bring replace the Bible.

We who embrace the Bible as God's inerrant Word have often failed to instruct our people in its extended message about angels, demons, and Satan. Many of our constituents are therefore not equipped to evaluate New Age angelology, for example. It is my prayer that this book will serve to inform us accurately about the spirit world. The Word of God must remain our standard, our norm, for evaluating all that people past or present say about angels. The Bible is as authoritative in its teaching about angels as it is in everything else in its pages.

The Annunciation

"And the angel answered and said to her, 'The Holy Spirit will come upon you, and the power of the Most High will overshadow you; and for that reason the holy offspring shall be called the Son of God . . .' And Mary said, 'Behold, the bondslave of the Lord; be it done to me according to your word.' And the angel departed from her." (Luke 1:35, 38)

CHAPTER THREE
Angels in the Bible

⟷

T HE PAGES OF SCRIPTURE abound with hundreds of references to angels. The Bible is our primary and only inspired source of information about these spirit beings; all other information about these heavenly creatures must be evaluated in light of God's Word.

In *A Dictionary of Angels* Gustav Davidson refers to several major extrabiblical sources of information on angels: the apocryphal New Testament books, the Book of Mormon, the Zohar (one of the major writings of the Cabala, a medieval Jewish mystic movement), the Old Testament Apocrypha and Pseudepigrapha, the Koran, and the Dead Sea Scrolls.[1]

Many religions include angels in their belief systems. Some of the world's major religious leaders claim to have received their original messages from angels (e.g., the founders of Islam and Mormonism).

In this chapter our primary concern is with the biblical descriptions of angels. Chapter 4 will discuss angelic activity—what angels do, according to the Bible. Here, however, we are concerned with what they are. In both of these chapters the subject is holy angels, not Satan, demons, or the Angel of the Lord. Separate attention is given later to these other personalities.

In the Bible angels are not mere figures of speech. Beginning in the first book of the Old Testament and continuing to the last book of the New Testament, angels appear, and they are always realities, not figments of imagination.

WHERE DO ANGELS COME FROM?

Some people believe angels come from within us. Juliana Dukes, who worked for Pfizer U.S. Pharmaceutical Group, found a stray and starving dog far out in the hills of New Mexico. Juliana was on her way to call on a customer, and she herself was almost lost. She found the dog's owner by calling the number on the collar tag. When the call came, the owners in Virginia were surprised and delighted that the dog had been found. They explained that the dog had strayed away two weeks earlier when they were vacationing in New Mexico.

Juliana said she learned a number of lessons from the experience. One was how important nametags for animals really are. But more importantly, she said "the best lesson was that angels come from within us."[2]

Is that where angels really come from, within us? No, the Bible presents a very different picture.

Angels did not always exist. Where, then, did they come from? God created them, just as He created man and animals. We cannot be sure when angels were created, but the fact that they were created is clear from the Bible. First, some passages speak of God as the Creator of all things. Paul's word to the Colossian Christians is an excellent example. Referring to God the Son he wrote, "And He is the image of the invisible God, the first-born of all creation. For by Him all things were created, both in the heavens and on earth, visible and invisible, whether thrones or dominions or rulers or authorities—all things have been created by Him and for Him" (Col. 1:15–16).

In rabbinic writings the words "rulers" and "authorities" described various orders of angels. These same descriptions are said to refer to those in "heavenly places" (Eph. 3:10), clearly referring to angels (cf. 6:12; Col. 2:10, 15).

Another all-inclusive passage that tells us God created the angels is John 1:3: "All things came into being by Him, and apart from Him nothing came

into being." Angels must certainly be included in such a sweeping statement. The One who brought everything into being is the "Word" (1:1),
who according to 1:14 is Jesus Christ: "The Word became flesh, and dwelt
among us."

In Psalm 148:2 the psalmist called on angels to praise the Lord, and
then in verse 5 he declared that they were created by God's command. No,
angels did not always exist; neither are they the products of evolution.
None of them evolved from anything. The God of the Bible created them,
not as male and female but as an order of beings. Each one was a direct
creation of God in a state of holiness. As we will see later, these holy angels were given a testing period and some fell.

Why, we might ask, did God create angels? What purpose or purposes did He have in mind for them? Since they were created "for" God
the Son (Col. 1:16), it follows that their chief task is to bring honor and
glory to their Creator. Since their creation, holy angels worship and serve
God (Ps. 103:20–21; Heb. 1:6). The apostle John's vision of angels around
the throne of God (Rev. 5:11–12) makes that abundantly clear.

No one knows how many angels exist. The number of angels now would
be the same, of course, as those who were created, since there is no death or
reproduction among angels. The number was fixed at the time of creation.
Some, especially in the Middle Ages, have tried to estimate their number.
For example, fourteenth-century cabalists arrived at the precise figure of
301,655,722. However, many today would regard this as a modest number.
Some scholars estimate there are billions or even trillions of angels.

The Bible gives only descriptions that point to a very large number.
The Old Testament speaks of the number as "the host of heaven" (1 Kings
22:19), "thousands upon thousands" (Ps. 68:17), and "myriads upon myriads" (Dan. 7:10).

Similar expressions occur in the New Testament: "a multitude of the
heavenly host" (Luke 2:13), "myriads of angels" (Heb. 12:22), and "myriads of myriads and thousands of thousands" (Rev. 5:11).

When did God create these vast numbers of angels? The Bible does
not give us a direct answer. We do know, though, that they were present
when God created the earth. That is what God told Job as He set him
straight on who did what in the world. God first asked the sufferer where

25

he was when God laid the earth's foundation (Job 38:4). Since Job certainly was not there, God told him who was there—"the sons of God," who at the sight of the created world "shouted for joy" (38:7). In the Bible the term "sons of God" usually, though not always, refers to angels (e.g., 1:6; 2:1; 38:7). How long before the creation of the earth were angels brought into existence? We do not know.

WHAT ARE ANGELS LIKE?

Angels do not reproduce after their kind. As stated, there are no more of them now than there were when God brought them into existence. That they do not procreate is clear from Jesus' word to the Sadducees, who did not believe in angels or the resurrection (Acts 23:8).

Some of the Sadducees came to Jesus with a question they thought would trap Him. Their question concerned a hypothetical man who died without children. Moses taught, they said, that in such a case the man's brother should marry the widow and raise a family (Matt. 22:23–24). The Sadducees asked Jesus whose wife this woman would be in the resurrection if she had married seven brothers, all of whom died.

Jesus saw through the hypocrisy of the Sadducees and answered them by saying, "In the resurrection they neither marry, nor are given in marriage, but are like angels in heaven" (22:30). God alone possesses immortality as an essential quality. He alone has it in and of Himself (1 Tim. 6:16). Angels' immortality, like man's, is similar to an endowment.

Scripture speaks often of holy and unholy angels, including Satan, as spirit beings. Therefore they do not possess material bodies, though at times angels appeared like humans.

Angels were often bright in appearance. The women who took spices to Jesus' tomb saw angels whose clothes "gleamed like lightning" (Luke 24:4 NIV), and Cornelius reported that the angel who appeared to him in a vision was "in shining clothes" (Acts 10:30 NIV). Even Satan seeks to conceal his identity by appearing "as an angel of light" (2 Cor. 11:14). The apostle John saw an angel whose "face was like the sun" (Rev. 10:1) and another angel who lit up the earth "by his splendor" (18:1 NIV). Perhaps these angels were reflecting some of the brilliance of God's glory.

DO ANGELS HAVE PERSONALITY?

Angels are not "its," powers, forces, figments of human imagination, or personifications of good and evil. They possess the essential elements of personality—intellect, emotion, and will, and the power of self-consciousness and self-determination. This means angels are aware of themselves. This is more than mere consciousness. Angels are able to objectify themselves, just as people are able to do so. Angels are also able to look to the future and plan an intelligent course of action. They have the power of choice. That is what self-determination means.

Though we are dealing in this chapter only with holy angels, it needs to be said that both holy and unholy angels, including Satan, are personalities. Granted, it is difficult for us to conceive of beings without physical bodies as persons. The only persons we have ever seen are those with physical bodies. Angels, of course, are spirit beings, just as surely as God is spirit; and they and God do not have physical bodies.

Angels have intellect, because they "long to look" (1 Pet. 1:12) into our salvation. They would love to understand how an absolutely holy God can accept a wretched sinner into His presence. At the birth of Christ holy angels gave audible praise to God (Luke 2:13); they were emotionally involved.

Since angels have a derived power from God, the power is limited. Only God is all-powerful; angels are not. However, they are "greater in might and power" than people (2 Pet. 2:11). In the Bible God gave an angel power to inflict physical harm on Herod because he did not glorify God (Acts 12:23). The psalmist said angels are "mighty in strength" (Ps. 103:20), yet they obey the voice of God's word. An angel sent by the Lord from heaven rolled away the huge stone from Jesus' grave (Matt. 28:2). Two other examples of the power of angels are recorded in the Book of Daniel. An angel rescued Shadrach, Meshach, and Abednego from the fiery furnace (Dan. 3:28), and an angel kept Daniel safe in the den of lions (6:22).

Since they are creatures, angels also possess limited knowledge. Though they are wise (2 Sam. 14:20), they are not all-knowing or omniscient as God is. Believers in this age are being observed by angels (1 Tim. 5:21), and the angels are learning about the wisdom of God (Eph. 3:10).

Also, angels are not omnipresent. They are not everywhere in their fullness at the same time as God is. Angels have spatial limitations. In the Bible they appear and disappear. They are said to be present, and then at other times there is no indication they are present.

DO ANGELS HAVE NAMES?

The most exhaustive list of angels' names is in Gustav Davidson's *Dictionary of Angels*. This work is the result of fifteen years of extensive research. Davidson arrived at his list of names from numerous sources, not just the Bible.

We are concerned here with names given to holy angels in the Bible. Very few are named there. Those who are named may be divided into three categories: those that are broad, general descriptions; those that are more specific; and those that are in various classifications or groupings of angels.

The natural place to begin listing the general names of angels is with the word *angel* itself. This word means "messenger," and it is used of both angelic (Rev. 16:1) and human (James 2:25) messengers. The context makes clear which is referred to.

Angels are also named "ministers." In Psalm 104:4 both names are ascribed to angels—"messengers" and "ministers." Angels are "ministering spirits" (Heb. 1:14) of God.

As stated earlier, "sons of God" is used of angels in Job 1:6; 2:1; and 38:7. Daniel the prophet called holy angels "watchers" (Dan. 4:13, 17, 23). The psalmist wrote of angels as "sons of the mighty" (Ps. 89:6). The "host of heaven" or God's "hosts" is used frequently of holy angels. Like a heavenly army, they are arrayed as a military force to carry out God's bidding (103:20–21). "God's camp" also describes angels (Gen. 32:2).

All the above are rather general terms used of angels. Some of them describe angelic ministry, while others reveal their nature. What follows below are specific names of angels.

The first appearance of specific names of angels comes from Daniel the prophet. He refers to Gabriel and Michael. These are the only two angelic beings given proper names in the Bible.

The name Gabriel means "mighty one of God" or "hero of God." Wherever this angel appears, he seems to always be delivering special messages from God to key people involved in accomplishing God's plan. Gabriel himself said he stood in the very "presence of God" (Luke 1:19). Yet each child of God has direct access to God and stands in His very presence as well, in and through the person of Jesus Christ.

Gabriel appeared, according to the biblical record, to Daniel, to Zacharias, and to Mary. To Daniel the prophet, Gabriel resembled a human being (Dan. 10:18), and therefore he called him "a man" (9:21).

Daniel received messages from God regarding the future from Gabriel. The prophet had seen a vision of a ram and a male goat (Dan. 8). Gabriel caused Daniel to understand both. The two-horned ram in the vision represented the Medo-Persian Empire (8:20). The "shaggy goat" represented the Grecian Empire under Alexander (8:21). This empire was later divided into four parts (8:15–22). All this was still future when Gabriel brought the message to Daniel.

This mighty angel also revealed to Daniel God's plan for the people of Israel while the nation was under Gentile rule. While the prophet was worshiping and praying to God, Gabriel came to him with the answer from God. It concerned the "seventy sevens" of years that God had in His plan for His people. The prophecy set the date of the Messiah's first coming as exactly 483 years after Artaxerxes's decree allowing Israel to rebuild the wall of the city of Jerusalem. The very last of these "seventy sevens" refers to a time still future after the present church age when God will bring unprecedented judgment on Israel and the world. After this, Christ will return and establish His kingdom on earth (Matt. 24:29–31; Rev. 19:1–6).

Zacharias, father of John the Baptist, was very fearful when he saw Gabriel (Luke 1:11–12). Mary, the mother of our Lord, was also greatly troubled, not so much perhaps at Gabriel's appearance but at what the heavenly messenger told her (Luke 1:30–34). Mary would give birth to Israel's Messiah and the world's Savior, yet she was a virgin.

Michael is perhaps the angel's name that is most familiar to many Christians. His name means "Who is like God?" and he is referred to as the "archangel" (Jude 9; also see 1 Thess. 4:16). Most believe there are other high-ranking angels, though Michael is the only one named an archangel (see Dan. 10:13). Somewhat in contrast to Gabriel, the heavenly messenger Michael is presented more as the guardian of Israel or the angelic military leader.

Daniel described Michael as "the great prince" (12:1), that is, a leader of the holy angels. Michael also acted as a guardian for the people of Israel (10:21). In a vision John saw Michael leading the angelic armies of heaven against Satan and his demons (Rev. 12:7). Michael had something to do with the burial of Moses (Jude 9), though we cannot be sure what it was. Though Michael was powerful and influential, he was totally dependent on the power of God for all he did.

The Bible speaks of specific angels who carry out specific directions from God, yet these are not given proper names. Examples of these are "the angel of the abyss" (Rev. 9:11) in John's vision on the Isle of Patmos. There was the angel with power over fire (14:18) and "the angel of the waters" (16:5). One particular unnamed angel will bind Satan in the future (20:1–2).

Three series of future judgments are yet to be poured out on the world—seal, trumpet, and bowl judgments. Angels will announce the arrival of each of the trumpet (Rev. 8–9) and bowl judgments (Rev. 16). Presumably these are holy angels who will be used of God to carry out His wrathful judgments on men and nations in the Tribulation.

The Bible also refers often to holy angels in various classifications or groupings. For example, "chosen angels" (1 Tim. 5:21) refers to holy angels. Paul challenged Timothy to live and minister according to biblical principles in light of the fact that he, Timothy, was seen by God and these angels. All holy angels then are the chosen or elect angels. In Revelation 3:5 the apostle John referred to God the Father and "His angels."

The word *cherubim* is the plural of *cherub*. Before his great sin Satan was a cherub (Ezek. 28:14, 16). The first reference to angels in the Bible is to the cherubim when they were placed at the entrance to the Garden of Eden (Gen. 3:24). Whenever they appear in Scripture, they seem to be involved in a protecting, defending position. At the Garden, after Adam and Eve had been driven out because of their sin, the cherubim were stationed with swords to guard the tree of life so no one would eat of it.

These holy creatures with spectacular appearance are seen also in the decorations of the mercy seat, the lid of the ark of the covenant (Exod. 25:17–22) in the innermost sanctuary of the tabernacle of Israel's worship. Here God's special glory was present. For this reason the writer of Hebrews referred to these angels as "cherubim of glory" (Heb. 9:5).

The prophet Ezekiel saw in a vision a chariot-like object that was moved by cherubim (Ezek. 10:15–20). They each had four faces and four wings. They were the same "living creatures" Ezekiel had seen earlier (10:15 NIV; see 1:4–24 NIV). They had the appearance of humans (1:5–6). Very likely, these cherubim are also the same creatures whom the apostle John saw and which he referred to as "four living creatures" (Rev. 4:6), though there are some differences between them.

Seraphim represent another special class of holy angels in Scripture, but they are referred to in only one passage. Isaiah 6:2–6 records Isaiah's vision of the throne room of God. Seraphim were hovering above the Lord on both sides of His throne. They called to each other, "Holy, Holy, Holy, is the LORD of hosts, the whole earth is full of His glory" (6:3). Obviously Isaiah saw at least two seraphim or perhaps even two groups of them, since he used the plural number (*seraphim* being the plural of *seraph*).

The scene of Isaiah's vision speaks of unceasing purification and worship of God. The word *seraph* means "burning" and thus speaks of burning devotion to God. Not only did the seraphim worship God; they also reminded the prophet of his need to be cleansed and to worship the Lord.

The apostle Paul wrote seven times of rulers, authorities, and principalities as a group of angels who govern in the universe. The same terms are used of both holy and unholy angels (Rom. 8:38; Eph. 1:21; 3:10; 6:12; Col. 1:16; 2:10, 15). The context determines which are in view. These angelic beings sometimes carry out their delegated power and authority through human leaders and at other times by themselves.

WHERE DO ANGELS "LIVE"?

The literature on Jewish life and customs referred to as the Judaica mentions seven heavens. The higher the heaven, the nearer one is to the place of complete ecstasy—the dwelling place of God.

In some books on occult philosophy, angelic rulers are assigned to these seven heavens:

first heaven—Gabriel,

second heaven—Zachariel and Raphael,

third heaven—Anahel,

fourth heaven—Michael,

fifth heaven—Sandalphon,

sixth heaven—Zachiel,

seventh heaven—Cassiel.[3]

The Bible, on the other hand, teaches there are only three heavens. About fourteen years before Paul wrote 2 Corinthians, he had a vision about which he wrote: "I know a man in Christ who fourteen years ago—whether in the body I do not know, or out of the body I do not know, God knows—such a man was caught up to the third heaven" (2 Cor. 12:2).

What are these three heavens, and in which of them do angels dwell? We know for a number of reasons from Scripture that holy angels do make their home in heaven. They are often described as "heavenly hosts." Jesus spoke of "angels in heaven" (Mark 13:32). An angel descended "from heaven" and rolled away the stone in front of Jesus' grave (Matt. 28:2). The apostle Paul wrote that even if an angel from heaven came and preached a foreign gospel, it should not be believed (Gal. 1:8).

We know, too, that when the eternal Son of God became man, He was for a little time lower than angels (Heb. 2:9). This means He passed through the realm of angels in order to take on a human nature so He could die for humankind. And when Jesus returned to God the Father, He "passed through the heavens" (Heb. 4:14). This would imply that angels dwell in the second heaven, though they have access to the third for special ministries (Isa. 6:3; Rev. 5:11; 7:11). The first heaven then is the atmospheric heaven, the second the stellar heaven and home of angels, and the third the abode of God.

Evangelicals are divided on whether holy angels have their home in the second heaven or the third. Some holy angels, it seems, do reside in God's presence. Examples might be those Isaiah saw in his vision (Isa. 6:1–6) and Gabriel, who stands in the presence of God (Luke 1:19).

Angels do not dwell where God dwells, though they may indeed have access there. We need to remember, too, that Satan desired to ascend to where God is (Isa. 14:13).

HOW DO ANGELS COMPARE WITH HUMANS?

Humans and angels have a number of similarities. Both are created by God. Both were created in a state of creaturely perfection. All that God made He pronounced very good. As we have seen, angels have personality. People possess personality as well. Angels and humankind sinned during their appointed times of probation. The angels sinned individually by following Satan in his great sin of pride and rebellion against God (Isa. 14:13–14). The human race sinned in and through Adam (Gen. 3; Rom. 5:12). Also both are to serve God, to be servants of the Most High God.

Neither angels nor humans are to be worshiped. Both are to worship God alone. John the apostle was so impressed and overwhelmed by what an angel showed him of the New Jerusalem that he fell down to worship the angel. Quickly the angel said to him, "Do not do that; I am a fellow servant of yours and of your brethren the prophets and of those who heed the words of this book; worship God" (Rev. 22:9). In his letter to the Colossian Christians Paul made it crystal clear that angels are never to be worshiped (Col. 2:18).

However, humans and angelic beings also have many dissimilarities. No divine grace was extended to angels who sinned by following Satan and his rebellion. Those who thus sinned were confirmed in their wickedness, and those who refused to follow Satan were confirmed in their holiness.

Angels are of a higher order of creation than people. In His incarnation Christ, the Redeemer, passed through the angelic order; He "was made for a little while lower than the angels" so that "He might taste death for everyone" (Heb. 2:9). To provide salvation for the world, Christ needed to become lower than angels for a while. Thus the human race is of a lower order of creation than angels. In the future eternal state, Christians will "judge" angels (1 Cor. 6:3), thus indicating that believers will occupy a higher position than angels.

Though people and angels are both creatures of God, there is nevertheless a great difference between them in relation to God. Angels are never said to be made in the image of God and after God's likeness, yet man is. Some believe angels were created in God's image,[4] though this is not specifically stated in Scripture. This idea is usually based on the fact that both have personalities, and personality is what is meant by the image of God. If that is all that is involved in the image of God, the conclusion would be a reasonable one. However, the meaning of the image of God in man involves much more, including man's responsibility to rule over the earth (Gen. 1:26). The image is also related to knowledge, righteousness, and holiness (Eph. 4:22–25; Col. 3:9–10; Rom. 8:29), as well as immortality.[5]

Angels do not propagate and are therefore distinct from people in this regard. They do not need to reproduce since they do not die as humans do. As indicated earlier, no salvation has been extended to angels. Holy angels observe salvation but do not fully comprehend it (1 Pet. 1:12). And we cannot understand it either. All we can say is it took a miracle to save our souls. But we can and should rejoice in it and share the gospel with our lives and our lips. It is the "power of God for salvation to everyone who believes" (Rom. 1:16).

An Angel Declares the Resurrection of Christ

"And entering the tomb, they saw a young man sitting at the right, wearing a white robe; and they were amazed. And he said to them, 'Do not be amazed; you are looking for Jesus the Nazarene, who has been crucified. He has risen; He is not here; behold, here is the place where they laid Him.'" (Mark 16:5–6)

CHAPTER FOUR
Angelic Activities in the Bible

—∞∞∞—

S EVENTEEN OLD TESTAMENT BOOKS make 108 references to angels, and 17 New Testament books refer to angels 165 times. Strangely, many questions about these spirit beings are not answered in the Bible. We do have enough information, though, to establish a biblical doctrine of angels and to evaluate the current craze, the angelmania, that is upon us.

The English word *angel* comes from the Hebrew word *malʾāk* and the Greek *angelos*. Both of these words mean "messenger." As noted earlier, the terms are used for spirit beings without physical bodies and for human messengers. The context tells us which is in view. We are concerned in this book only with the messengers who are spirit beings. In this chapter holy angels are our concern, not Satan and demons. The latter two will be discussed in subsequent chapters of this book.

Except for the first in the list of angelic activities which follows, there is no significance in the order in which these activities are presented. God's ministering spirits are discussed first because their work of ministering is their primary role. As ministering spirits these messengers carry out God's bidding.

Limited examples of the activities named will be cited. There is some overlap in the activities. More activities could be added; only the major ones are included. Ministries performed by the Angel of the Lord are not included here because chapter 5 is devoted to this angel's identification and ministry.

MINISTERING SPIRITS OF GOD

As stated, the very meaning of the Hebrew and Greek words translated "angel" reveals their chief assignment. The writer of Hebrews affirms that the holy angels are "ministering spirits, sent out to render service for the sake of those who will inherit salvation" (Heb. 1:14). They are God's "ministers" (1:7).

We certainly do not know all the specific ways in which holy angels minister to believers, but we are assured in Scripture that they do minister to God's children. Many of the following activities serve as illustrations of some of the ways they minister.

The ministries to and for Christ by angels is another great area of ministry not to be overlooked. Again, the Book of Hebrews stresses these activities, thereby highlighting Christ's superiority to the angels.

CARRYING MESSAGES FROM GOD

Abraham's nephew, Lot, lived among the wicked Sodomites (Gen. 19). God sent two angels to deliver Lot from destruction. They told Lot to take his wife and daughters and get out of the city before God's judgment fell on it.

The men of Sodom intended to sexually molest Lot's two guests. Neither the Sodomites nor Lot realized at first that the two were angels of God appearing as men. These angels, faithful in their service to God, surrounded Lot until he was safe outside the wicked city. These same two angels not only carried God's message to Lot but also were used of God to bring judgment on the wicked Sodomites.

The God-fearing Cornelius, a centurion of an Italian regiment, "saw in a vision an angel of God" (Acts 10:3). The angel spoke to Cornelius directly and specifically. A special message was on its way. The angel told Cornelius to dispatch some men to Joppa to seek out Simon called Peter. The angel even gave specific instruction on where Peter could be found.

When the angel concluded his message, he left. Cornelius wasted no time doing precisely as the angel told him. He explained the assignment to his men and sent them to Joppa.

Before the three men (two servants and a soldier, 10:7) who had been sent by Cornelius arrived at Peter's house, God gave Peter a vision. A sheet came down to earth on which were all kinds of four-footed animals, crawling creatures, and birds. A voice told Peter to kill and eat them. He refused to do so because the animals on the sheet were unclean according to Jewish law. The voice said Peter should not call unclean what God had cleansed, and then the sheet was lifted up toward heaven.

About that time, after God had prepared Peter, the three men arrived. They rehearsed what the angel had told Cornelius and said that Peter was invited to come to Cornelius's house and give him God's message. Although Peter was a Jew and Jews did not associate that way with Gentiles, he went and told Cornelius and his relatives and friends all about Christ's death, resurrection, and the commission Christ gave to the apostles. As Peter spoke, the Holy Spirit fell on the Gentiles as He had in Jerusalem on the Day of Pentecost. All this took place because an angel gave God's message to Cornelius.

GIVING GUIDANCE AND INSTRUCTION

At the bidding of his father, Isaac, Jacob left Beersheba and headed for Haran to find a wife. One night as he slept with a stone for a pillow, he had a dream in which he saw a ladder reaching from earth to heaven. Angels of God were ascending and descending the ladder (Gen. 28:10–12). In Jacob's dream God stood beside him. The Lord assured Jacob that he was the God-appointed heir of the covenant given to Abraham and Isaac.

Jacob was convinced that God was at work in him and would use him mightily. The very place where he slept, saw the ladder and the angels, and heard God's message was sacred to him. Jacob saw the place as the very gateway to heaven through which angels passed to do their earthly chores. He changed the name of that place from Luz to Bethel (28:17), which means "the house of God."

Later God told Jacob to go back from Haran to his homeland (31:11, 13).

When he was on his way home, "the angels of God" met him again and assured him of God's presence with him (32:1–2). God told Moses He would send an angel to guide the Israelites through the wilderness (Exod. 23:20; 32:34) to the land of Canaan (23:23; 33:2). Here a single angel led the entire nation of Israel for forty years.

The New Testament includes similar examples of holy angels giving guidance and instruction from God to man. For example, Philip was led to the Ethiopian eunuch by instruction from "an angel of the Lord" (Acts 8:26). The angel gave him specific directions with vivid descriptions of conditions around the place. This angel must have known when the man from Ethiopia would be passing by there. He knew too what he would be doing—reading from the prophecy of Isaiah. God sent his angel to bring Philip and the court official from Ethiopia together so that the Ethiopian might hear the gospel and become a child of God.

DELIVERING FROM DANGER

As the infant church, begun on the Day of Pentecost, grew and expanded, the unbelieving Jewish authorities opposed the apostles and early Christians. Out of jealousy the high priest and the Sadducees had the apostles put in the public jail (Acts 5:17–18).

During the night as the apostles slept, an angel not only opened the gates of the jail and took the apostles out but also told them what they were to do. They were to give to the temple authorities the same message they preached before they were incarcerated.

But when the apostles did this, they were again brought before the unbelieving Jewish leaders and warned not to speak anymore in the name of Jesus. The apostles listened politely and then proceeded to do exactly what they were told not to do (5:21–42).

On another occasion Peter was put in prison by Herod Agrippa's order. The wicked king already had had James, John's brother, put to death. He saw that this pleased the Jewish leaders, so he arrested Peter also and assigned four squads of four soldiers each to guard him. Herod planned to bring Peter before the people after the Passover and then no doubt have him put to death.

A band of believers heard about this and began a concerted prayer effort. Peter, bound with chains, was sleeping soundly between two of the guards. Suddenly an angel of the Lord appeared to him. A bright light shone in the dark dingy place. Arousing Peter from sleep, the angel told him to get up quickly. Peter thought he was seeing a vision. He obeyed the angel, and when he did, the chains that bound him fell off (12:1–7).

Then the angel told Peter to put his cloak around him, put his sandals on, and follow him. Peter did so, still thinking he was having a vision. He followed the angel past two guards and watched the huge iron gates open miraculously.

Once outside, the angel disappeared just as suddenly as he had appeared. When Peter realized what had happened, he went to Mary's house, John's mother, and discovered a prayer meeting for him was in session. Those praying could not believe their prayers were answered (12:8–17).

When Herod discovered all this, he had the guards led off to execution. God later sent another angel, or perhaps the same one, who struck Herod, and Herod died because he would not acknowledge the God of heaven. So the one who had God's servants killed was himself killed by one of the Lord's angelic servants (12:18–23).

VIEWING HUMAN AFFAIRS

The Bible records several examples of angels observing the lives and activities of God's people.

Paul the apostle was setting forth himself as an example of doing Christ-honoring Christian service. He wrote, "God has exhibited us apostles last of all, as men condemned to death; because we have become a spectacle to the world, both to angels and to men" (1 Cor. 4:9). This observation by angels indicates their interest in the work of redemption, even though they are not recipients of it.

A similar reminder was given to the women in the Corinthian church. They, too, were being watched by angels. Because of this, they were to cover their heads at worship (11:10). Why holy angels were concerned about women's head-coverings is not clear.

Paul wrote to the believers in Ephesus that his ministry would cause angelic beings to see the wisdom of God in His ways with people. "Rulers and the authorities in the heavenly places" (Eph. 3:10) refers to angels. In rabbinic thought these terms, as well as "power and dominion" (1:21), described order and rank among angels.

The apostle solemnly charged Timothy, his son in the faith, about local church affairs, and Paul made this charge not only "in the presence of God and of Christ Jesus" but also before "His chosen angels" (1 Tim. 5:21). This too indicates angelic observance of human affairs.

Peter wrote that human salvation is something into which "angels long to look" (1 Pet. 1:12). The Greek verb used here (*parakryptō*) means to stoop or bend down (or stretch forward the head) to look so as to get a better view of something. The same word is used to describe the apostles' search for the body of Jesus at the tomb of Joseph of Arimathea (Luke 24:12; John 20:5).

Finally, God's angels rejoice when sinners accept the Savior as their Substitute for sin (Luke 15:10).

PROTECTING GOD'S PEOPLE

In the Bible angels did more than deliver messages and observe human affairs. They also were personally involved in protecting God's people in times of great need.

Two familiar incidents recorded in the Old Testament illustrate this work of God's angels very well. The first of these is the fiery-furnace episode of Shadrach, Meshach, and Abednego. We cannot help but wonder what they thought would happen to them. They made it clear that whether God would deliver them from the furnace or let them die by the flames, they would not serve Nebuchadnezzar's gods (Dan. 3:16–18). The king soon discovered that not only did the three not burn in his furnace, but a fourth person was with them. He said the fourth had an appearance "like a son of the gods" (3:25). This was God's special agent, a holy angel, sent to protect His servants.

Some years later Daniel refused to worship pagan gods, just as his three friends had done. Darius, the king, was caught in a trap and in order to save face he allowed his friend Daniel to be thrown to the lions. The king could not wait until morning to see what had happened to Daniel.

Had Daniel's God protected him or not? God had saved Daniel, and He did it by sending His angel and shutting the lions' mouths (6:22). As already noted, centuries earlier an angel guarded (and guided) Israel in the wilderness wanderings (Exod. 23:20).

We have already observed from the New Testament how holy angels delivered the apostles and Peter from prison on two separate occasions (Acts 5:17–24; 12:3–12). Those angelic deliverances also illustrate God's protection of His own.

As Paul was being taken to Rome as a prisoner, the ship he was on encountered a severe storm and the lives of everyone on board were in danger. Paul stood boldly before them all and gave this message: "There shall be no loss of life among you . . . for this very night an angel of the God to whom I belong and whom I serve stood before me, saying, 'Do not be afraid, Paul; you must stand before Caesar; and behold, God has granted you all those who are sailing with you'" (27:22–24). Here an angel encouraged Paul and kept alive everyone on the ship during the terrifying storm.

PROVIDING STRENGTH AND ENCOURAGEMENT

Elijah was running from the wicked Jezebel, wife of Ahab. After about one day's journey into the desert the prophet came to a juniper tree and begged God to let him die (1 Kings 19:3–4). As he prayed, Elijah fell asleep. He was awakened by an angel touching him and telling him to get up and eat.

When Elijah got up as the angel told him to, he saw by his head a cake of bread baked over hot coals and a jar of water. He ate it and then lay down again. A second time the strange creature came and touched Elijah, and told him to get up and eat. The angel had prepared a meal for the prophet and provided water for him to drink. Elijah's physical strength was restored for forty days and forty nights (19:5–8).

The angel Gabriel told the fearful Zacharias that his wife, Elizabeth, would have a son whose name was to be John (Luke 1:8–9, 11–13). Zacharias was from the priestly tribe of Levi, and Elizabeth was a descendant of Aaron. Presumably they both were about sixty years old at the time. The angel ministered to Zacharias by calming his fears at what he saw and heard.

The same angel ministered to the Virgin Mary in a similar way (1:27–28, 30–31). Mary too was fearful, and she wondered, How could I, a virgin, ever be pregnant? The heavenly messenger said to her, "Do not be afraid, Mary; for you have found favor with God. And behold, you will conceive in your womb, and bear a son, and you shall name Him Jesus" (1:30–31). Like Elijah and Zacharias, she, too, was encouraged by an angel.

EXECUTING JUDGMENT

In reviewing the history of the Israelites, the psalmist Asaph gave this description of the plagues God inflicted on the Egyptians: "He sent upon them His burning anger, Fury, and indignation, and trouble, a band of destroying angels" (Ps. 78:49). The angel who led and protected the Israelites in the wilderness was also involved in helping them destroy the inhabitants of Canaan (Exod. 32:2).

Jesus gave and then explained to His disciples the parable of the wheat and the tares (Matt. 13:24–30, 37–43). The gathering and burning of the tares, He said, would involve Him and His angels. "The Son of Man will send forth His angels, and they will gather out of His kingdom all stumbling blocks, and those who commit lawlessness, and will cast them into the furnace of fire; in that place there shall be weeping and gnashing of teeth" (13:41–42).

On another occasion Jesus made a similar announcement. He said the Son of Man would come to the earth "in the glory of His Father with His angels; and will then recompense every man according to his deeds" (16:27). In other words, the angels of God will assist Him in His work of judgment in the future.

The Book of Revelation records a number of examples of angels executing divine judgment. John the apostle saw four angels in control of the elements of nature on the earth (Rev. 7:1). He also saw in his vision of Armaggedon an angel with power over fire (14:18). Seven angels each blew a trumpet to announce a series of judgments (chaps. 8–9). An eighth angel came in John's vision and held a golden censer. "Much incense was given to him, that he might add it to the prayers of all the saints upon the golden altar which was before the throne" (8:3). When each angel blew his trumpet, awful divine punishment by the wrath of God came on the world.

Another outstanding example of angelic involvement in the outpouring of future judgment is in Revelation 15–16. Again, John saw seven angels who held seven bowls of divine wrath to be poured out upon the world. In turn, each one emptied his bowl of God's wrath on people and nations.

Many other angels are mentioned by John in Revelation. God will employ them to carry out the world's rendezvous with divine judgment in the future Tribulation.

PRAISING GOD

One of the chief activities of holy angels is giving worship to God. The Bible repeatedly speaks of angels praising the Lord.

The psalmist called on his own heart to praise God (Ps. 103:1). Then he begged the angels to bless Him. In doing so, he described these angels as "mighty in strength," those who "perform His word" and who are constantly obeying "the voice of His word" (103:20).

In Isaiah's vision the seraphim were occupied constantly with worship of God (Isa. 6:1–7). One of the seraphim cried out to another, saying, "Holy, Holy, Holy is the LORD of hosts" (6:3). The seraphim each had six wings—two covered their face, two their feet, and two were used to fly. One of the angels in Isaiah's vision flew to the prophet and took a burning coal from the altar in the vision, touched Isaiah's mouth, and told him he was cleansed and his sin forgiven (6:6–7). The angel did not forgive him. God alone forgave him, and the angel simply announced the forgiveness to Isaiah.

Christ's superiority to angels is stressed by the writer of Hebrews in the beginning of the book. God the Father never said to an angel "You are My Son" (Heb. 1:5), but the Lord Jesus Christ is the eternal Son of God. Angels were given the assignment of worshiping Christ the Son of God when He came into the world. "And let all the angels of God worship Him" (1:6), they were told. They did and continue to do so.

John described angels as "four living creatures" (Rev. 4:8), which are probably the same as the creatures in Ezekiel's vision in Ezekiel 1 and the cherubim in Ezekiel 10. They never cease saying essentially what the seraphim said in Isaiah's vision: "Holy, holy, holy, is the LORD God, the Almighty, who was and who is to come" (Rev. 4:8).

In Revelation 5:12 an innumerable company of angels were heard saying, "Worthy is the Lamb." This paean of praise resulted from the fact that
Christ, the Lamb of God, was worthy to open the sealed book, which no
one else was worthy to open.

The angels of God serve as examples for us as God's children to never
cease to worship God the Father, God the Son, and God the Holy Spirit.
Instead of always asking God to bless us in all our needs, we need to bless
Him, and praise Him even when we are hurting and things are not going
our way. There simply is no more important activity in which we can be
involved than the worship of our great God.

Never does Scripture give any sanction to humans praying to angels
or worshiping them. To the contrary, there are injunctions against such
behavior. Those who did worship angels in the early days of the church
were rebuked sharply by Paul (Col. 2:18). On one occasion the apostle
John himself fell down and began to worship an angel. But that angel
promptly rebuked him. The angel said, "Do not do that, I am a fellow
servant of yours and of your brethren the prophets and of those who
heed the words of this book; worship God" (Rev. 22:9; also see 19:10).

GUARDING BELIEVERS

The ministry of holy angels on behalf of God's people is clearly taught or
implied in Scripture. The ministries we have surveyed lend support to
the reality of guardian angels.

Some secular theorists today go far beyond Scripture in assigning
guardian angels to the planets in our solar system. Seven of these angels
are named, along with the planet over which each one is said to preside.
Rahatiel is said to be the chief angel of the planets. Raphael is over the
sun, Gabriel is over the moon, and five of the planets each has a named
angel: Michael is over Mercury, Aniel over Venus, Samel over Mars, Zadkiel
over Jupiter, and Kafziel over Saturn.[1]

The term "guardian angels" does not appear in Scripture. That, of
course, does not mean such beings do not exist. Though the term is sometimes used to speak of angelic ministry to adults, it is usually used with
reference to infants and young children. The familiar Christian artist's

visualization of one or more angels rescuing a child from great danger portrays this concept.

Some believe each child has one holy angel assigned to him or her by God. Others believe each child has more than one angel. Still others believe that holy angels in general have the care of infants and children as their assignment rather than one or more specific angels being responsible for each child. The key verse in support of guardian angels for infants and children is Matthew 18:10. To His disciples Jesus illustrated the need for childlike faith as He called a child to His side. He then said to them, "See that you do not despise one of these little ones, for I say to you, that their angels in heaven continually behold the face of My Father who is in heaven."

Rather than one or more angels attending each child, this verse may mean that angels carry out a general ministry to them by representing them before God, as they appear in God's presence (beholding His "face") in heaven.[2]

Do angels minister to adult believers also? Indeed they do! The writer of Hebrews affirmed this clearly when he wrote that "ministering spirits [are] sent out to render service for the sake of those who will inherit salvation" (Heb. 1:14). The question is not, "Do angels do this?" but rather, "When does this ministry begin?" We are not told specifically, but it seems natural that it would begin as soon as life begins.

Further support for the ministry of guardian angels over God's people is in both the Old and New Testaments. Here are some specific verses bearing on the subject. We have referred to some of these already in this chapter.

When the prophet Elijah was fleeing from Jezebel for his life, he lay down to sleep under a juniper tree in the desert. There an angel came and ministered to him (1 Kings 19:5).

The psalmist said the Lord would give a host of His angels charge over His people to "guard" them in all their ways (Ps. 91:11) and protect them from harm (91:12–13).

Daniel told Darius that an angel kept him safe while he was in the lions' den overnight. "My God sent His angel and shut the lions' mouths, and they have not harmed me" (Dan. 6:22).

After the wise men who worshiped Baby Jesus left to return home, "an angel of the Lord appeared to Joseph in a dream" (Matt. 2:13). The angel told him to take Mary and the baby Jesus and escape to Egypt. After Herod died, an angel of the Lord appeared again to Joseph, telling him to return to his homeland (2:19–20).

As Lockyer points out, knowing angels guard us can ease our concerns in life. "It is to be feared that the presence and power of Angels are not as real to us as they should be. While we have no way of knowing how often our feet are directed into right paths, or how often we are guarded from harm, seen or unseen, or how subject we are to angelic suggestion, our invisible companions are ever at hand. They form our protective shield, and over and above them is the everlasting God and Father they serve and we love. So why should we charge our souls with care?"[3] As we think of guardian angels watching over us, we need to be sure we keep our eyes on the God who sent them, not on the angels themselves.

Summary

The Bible clearly presents angels as God's worshipers and messengers— those who carry out His bidding, assisting Him and His people. They themselves never sinned and therefore have never experienced God's saving grace, but their ministries toward humans who did sin and have been redeemed are abundant.

Two of the angels' many activities are their ministry for God and their praise of God. Besides these two chief functions in relation to God, we saw that they have many responsibilities in relation to people: delivering messages from God to individuals, guiding and instructing God's people, delivering them from danger and death, observing human affairs, protecting God's people, providing strength and encouragement for God's special servants, and executing divine judgment on the deserving.

COMPARISON

Much of present-day angelmania activity cannot be found in the Bible. People, no doubt in all sincerity, assign powers and abilities to angels

beyond what the Bible teaches. These either find no basis at all in the Bible or are exaggerations and distortions of what the Bible says.

The twelve Zodiac signs are said to have angelic governors, who watch over the months of the year, as follows:

Angel	Month	Zodiac Sign
Cambiel or Gabriel	January	Aquarius (the Water Carrier)
Barchiel	February	Pisces (the Fishes)
Malahidael	March	Aries (the Ram)
Asmodel	April	Taurus (the Bull)
Ambriel	May	Gemini (the Twins)
Muriel	June	Cancer (the Crab)
Verchiel	July	Leo (Lion)
Hamaliel	August	Virgo (the Virgin)
Zuriel or Uriel	September	Libra (the Scales)
Barbiel	October	Scorpio (the Scorpion)
Advachiel or Adnachiel	November	Sagittarus (the Archer)
Hanael	December	Capricorn (the Goat)[4]

Many believe there are certain angels for each day of the week and even each hour of the day and night. Some even believe angels are assigned to animals. Over tame beasts there is the angel Behemiel, while Thegri is the angel assigned to wild beasts. Birds, too, are under angelic supervision, we are told. Arael is the angel over birds. The dove, however, is the only creature who has its own angel, namely, Alphun.

A woman reported that she was visited by four angels one night as she contemplated all the things she still needed to do before she died. She said she knew the angels were there in the room with her because her golden retriever

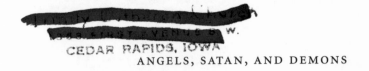
saw them. And she said she knew that because the dog nosed one of the angels out of his way so he could go to sleep on his favorite spot in the room.[5]

Some angels take care of plants and trees. These hold the key as to how they are formed. A so-called nature spirit builds plants and trees from the plans formulated by angels.

Angels are currently watching over countries, states, and even cities, according to many people. These are called Archons or "rulers." These spirit beings help guide the primary mission of that place so as to make it more successful in realizing its goal.

The weather and seasons of the year are controlled by angels, some insist.

Present-day angel theorists insist angels have their own celestial alphabets. These are variations of the Hebrew alphabet. "Who knows what masterpieces some may have written for the pleasure of the angelic realm?"[6]

People frequently report having received some communication from angels. This takes varied forms. It may be simply an extremely strong feeling, the communication of certain facts, or a physical intervention by an angel's hand or body. Usually this latter form comes to keep the person from danger or even death. Some report they have heard angel voices giving instruction. They urge all who hear these voices to obey them.

CONCLUSION

What we believe about angels must be based on the Word of God. All our doctrines should not be built on an experience someone claims to have had. Simply because someone says he or she saw or heard an angel does not mean what they saw or heard was in fact an angel. It is not unusual, for example, to have a dream in which "people" are seen and voices "heard." I have had such dreams myself. When we awake, we discover that what we saw was real only in our dreams.

Angels continue to be God's ministering spirits. There can be no doubt about that. But do they minister in the same way they did when the Bible was in the making?

We do not know which specific ministries of angels continue today and which do not. We can be sure that some do not, but does that mean none of them do? Hardly. But since the canon of Scripture is closed, angels are no longer being used of God to give His revelation to people. If angels were still giving inspired messages, this would mean the Scriptures are not complete.

Are angels still opening prison doors as they did for the apostles? Do those who are innocent but judged guilty escape the electric chair or lethal injection by the intervention of an angel? We do not put criminals in fiery furnaces or dens of lions today, but do these same kinds of deliverances occur today?

Since we can be sure that some activities of angels no longer occur, others may be imagined as taking place but actually do not.

It is also strikingly strange that those reporting and recording angelic citings and voices rarely, if ever, see or hear them meting out judgment on offenders. Instead, they are seen with happy, helpful messages, always offering assistance to individuals. Yet in the Bible angels often carried out God's judgments, and they will do so in the future. Why not now?

If we would each keep our focus on Jesus, we would be fulfilling the biblical mandate. He is the living Word of God. Must we know if an angel (or angels) is involved in particular areas of our lives? We know God has promised to care for us. Is that not enough? What difference does it make whether we "see" or "hear" an angel?

Focusing on angels and what they can or cannot do keeps us from being occupied with Jesus. Though the Bible has much to say about angels, at no time were people intended to be caught up with angelmania. We are to focus on the Lord, not angels. Angels have never witnessed for Christ. That is our task. Angels have never prayed for lost souls. That is our job. Angels do not distribute the Word of God to people either. That is a privilege God has given us.

The songwriter put it all in perspective in this song:

Holy, Holy, Is What the Angels Sing

There is singing up in heaven such as we have never known,
Where the angels sing the praises of the Lamb upon the throne;
Their sweet harps are ever tuneful and their voices always clear,
Oh, that we might be more like them while we serve the Master here.

Refrain:
Holy, holy, is what the angels sing,
And I expect to help them make the courts of heaven ring;
But when I sing redemption's story, they will fold their wings,
For angels never felt the joys that our salvation brings.

Then the angels stand and listen, for they cannot join that song,
Like the sound of many waters, by that happy, bloodwashed throng;
For they sing about great trials, battles fought and vict'ries won,
And they praise their great Redeemer, who hath said to them, "Well done."

So, although I'm not an angel, yet I know that over there
I will join a blessed chorus that the angels cannot share;
I will sing about my Saviour, who upon dark Calvary
Freely pardoned my transgressions, died to set a sinner free.[7]

Balaam and the Angel of the Lord
"Then the LORD opened the eyes of Balaam, and he saw the Angel of the LORD standing in
the way with his drawn sword in his hand; and he bowed all the way to the ground."
(Num. 22:31)

CHAPTER FIVE
The Angel Called God

———ऒ———

A LL THE ANGELS in the Bible, including Satan and his demons, were created by God. They were all in a state of perfection, but Satan sinned and led a host of the angelic beings with him who became demons. All angels were created by God except one—the Angel of the Lord (or the Angel of Yahweh).

This One is clearly distinguished from all the angelic beings in a number of ways, yet he is called an "angel." At times he is distinguished from God, and at other times he seems to be identified with God.

Besides being called "the angel of the LORD" (e.g., Gen. 16:7), he is also referred to as "My presence" (Exod. 33:14), "captain of the host of the LORD" (Josh. 5:14), the "messenger of the covenant" (Mal. 3:1, literal translation), and the "I Am" (Exod. 3:14).

Before we can attempt to identify this most unusual angel, we need to see from the Scriptures what he did.

MINISTRIES OF THE ANGEL OF THE LORD

A number of people were privileged not only to see this most unique angel but also to receive messages from him. Each time this Angel appeared, he performed a special ministry.

The Ministry of the Angel of the Lord to Hagar

God had promised Abraham He would make of him a great nation and his descendants would be like the stars in the sky and the sand by the seashore in number (Gen. 12:1–3). But years had passed and he and Sarah still had no children.

Sarah decided the fault was with herself, so she told Abraham to take Hagar as his wife and perhaps she would bear children for Sarah. Abraham agreed and Hagar became pregnant. Sarah then became terribly depressed and despised Hagar, even though Hagar had only done what her master told her to do. So Sarah treated Hagar harshly, causing Hagar to leave. As she was making her way back to Egypt, her homeland, the angel found her in the desert, lonely, forsaken, despised, and pregnant (16:1–7).

The Angel of the Lord asked Hagar where she had been and where she was going (16:8). Hagar replied that she was running away from her mistress. Then the Angel told Hagar to go back to Sarah and Abraham and submit to their authority (16:9). In addition, the angel comforted Hagar with predictions concerning the future. He told Hagar she was pregnant and the child, a son, would be named Ishmael. The angel also told Hagar what Ishmael would be like, how he would treat others, and how they would treat him (16:10–12).

Immediately Hagar recognized that the One whom she saw and who spoke with her was greater than any creature on earth. This One could foretell the future. Impressed, Hagar responded by saying, "Thou art a God who sees; for she said, 'Have I even remained alive here after seeing Him?' " (16:13). Of note is the fact that she called the angel "God."

The Ministry of the Angel of the Lord to Abraham

Sarah eventually did bear a son to Abraham. His name was Isaac. In obedience to God, Abraham took Isaac, his beloved son and heir, up to Mount Moriah and bound him to the altar he erected there. Following God's instructions, Abraham was about to plunge a knife into his boy's body and offer him as a sacrifice to God. But the Angel of the Lord called out to Abraham, "Do not stretch out your hand against the lad, and do nothing to him; for now I know that you fear God, since you have not withheld your only son, from Me" (Gen. 22:12). The words of the Angel of the Lord in verse 15 are said in verse 16 to have been spoken by the Lord.

The angel also said to Abraham, "Because you have done this thing, and have not withheld your son, your only son, indeed I will greatly bless you, and I will greatly multiply your seed as the stars of the heavens, and as the sand which is on the seashore; and your seed shall possess the gate of their enemies" (22:16–17). Of interest is the fact that the angel predicted exactly what God Himself had earlier predicted.

The Ministry of the Angel of the Lord to Jacob

A number of years after the angel's ministry at the near death of Isaac, his son Jacob got a direct message from "the angel of God" (Gen. 31:11). Jacob's father-in-law, Laban, had cheated him and turned against him. However, God protected Jacob and ministered to him through the most unique of all angels.

Jacob had a dream in which this "angel of God" told him to return home to the land of his birth. Leah and Rachel, Jacob's wives for whom he had served Laban fourteen years, agreed that their father had lied and cheated Jacob, and that all Jacob had acquired of cattle and wealth was his. They agreed too that they should all go back to Jacob's homeland.

Of course Jacob had himself engaged in deceit earlier (Gen. 27). Now he experienced compounded deception from Laban, and yet God protected him, and the Angel of God ministered to him at a most critical time of need. It is striking that "the angel of God" (31:11) said, "I am the God of Bethel" (31:13).

As Jacob followed the instructions the angel gave him, he experienced another encounter with this most unique angel. On the way home he camped one night along the Jabbok River. Before he made camp, he sent his family and belongings across the river.

That night as he was alone, he had a strange experience. "A man [who] wrestled with him until daybreak" (32:24) dislocated the socket of Jacob's thigh and caused him to limp as he tried to walk. The "man" asked Jacob his name, and when Jacob told him his name, the "man" changed it to Israel (32:27–28). The "man" blessed Jacob there, and then Jacob named the place Peniel (32:29–30), which means "the face of God." Jacob called this "man" God, for he said, "I have seen God face to face" (32:30). The prophet Hosea was led by the Holy Spirit to tell us the "man" whom Jacob saw that night was "the angel," and Hosea also said Jacob struggled "with God" (Hos. 12:3–4).

The Ministry of the Angel of the Lord to Moses

Centuries after this special angel's ministry to Jacob, the same angel appeared to Moses when he was herding sheep near Horeb, the mountain of God in the Sinai Peninsula. At that time Moses was an exile from the Egypt an court, keeping his father-in-law, Jethro's, sheep.

All of a sudden one of the many thorn trees in the wilderness became engulfed in flames. That in itself was not totally uncommon because of the extreme dryness and heat common to the area. What was most unusual, however, was the fact that though the tree burned furiously, it was not burned up.

As Moses turned to look at the tree more carefully, he saw and heard "the angel of the LORD" (Exod. 3:2). Still inquisitive, Moses tried to determine why the fire was not burning up the tree. As he proceeded, God warned him not to come closer. Furthermore, he was to take off his sandals because he was standing on holy ground (3:4–5). The angel whom Moses saw then identified himself as "the God of Abraham, the God of Isaac, and the God of Jacob" (3:6). At this, Moses hid his face because he was rightly afraid to look at God.

The message God then gave Moses was comforting indeed. God told Moses He had not forgotten His promises to Israel. He had seen and cared about their affliction in Egypt. The Lord assured Moses that Pharaoh would let God's people go and that Moses would be His representative to cause it to happen (3:7–10).

The Ministry of the Angel of the Lord to the Israelites

God's people had backslidden. They had continued to be disobedient to Him. In New Testament terms we would say they were out of fellowship with God. They were not walking in the light as God is in the light. Instead, they were walking in darkness. The most outstanding of their sins was their refusal to tear down the pagan altars in the land and to turn from idolatry.

The message of the Angel of the Lord was clear enough to Israel's leaders: "I brought you up out of Egypt and led you into the land which I have sworn to your fathers; and I said, 'I will never break My covenant with you, and as for you, you shall make no covenant with the inhabitants of this land; you shall tear down their altars.' But you have not obeyed Me" (Judg. 2:1–2).

The angel added that the idol-worshipers of the land would not be driven out but instead would become like thorns in the sides of the Israelites (2:3). When the Israelites heard these words, they wept bitterly and worshiped God by sacrificing to Him (2:4–5).

The Ministry of the Angel of the Lord to Gideon

Because of Israel's sin in the days of Gideon the Lord gave them over to the Midianites (Judg. 6:1–6). When the Israelites finally cried to the Lord, He graciously sent them a prophet (6:7–8) to whom the angel of the Lord appeared and gave instructions for his task (6:11–16). God promised Gideon He would be with him as he carried out his commission.

Gideon prepared a sacrifice to God in response to his call. The angel instructed him concerning the sacrifice and miraculously ignited the fire to consume it and then departed. When Gideon realized the Angel of the Lord had visited him, he feared he might die, but he was assured he would not (6:17–24). The Angel of the Lord, who spoke to Gideon in verse 12, is then referred to as the Lord, who spoke to him in verse 14 and 16. And the Angel of the Lord, who addressed Gideon in verse 20, is the Lord, who spoke to Gideon in verse 23.

The Ministry of the Angel of the Lord to Manoah and His Wife

All whom the Angel of the Lord visited were honored by God, including Manoah and his wife, the parents of Samson.

The special angelic messenger from the Lord announced to Manoah's wife, who was barren, that she would give birth to a son, who would in time deliver Israel from the Philistines (Judg. 13:2–5). The angel also appeared to Manoah, who called Him "the man of God" (13:8); and both Manoah and his wife called Him "the man" (13:10–12), apparently because of his human appearance. When Manoah and his wife sacrificed a grain offering to the Lord, the Angel of the Lord ascended in the flame of the altar (13:20). Manoah then said they had seen God (13:22).

Other Manifestations of the Angel of the Lord

On a number of other occasions the angel of the Lord is referred to briefly. For example, this unique "angel of God" was in the pillar of a cloud and the pillar of fire that led Israel through the wilderness (Exod. 14:19). Yet this same one is called the Lord (13:21).

Even Balaam's donkey was confronted by this heavenly messenger (Num. 22:22–27). The righteous Judge pronouncing judgment on David's sin in numbering Israel was also the Angel of the Lord (2 Sam. 24:16–17). The same One was also involved in the slaying of 185,000 Assyrians (2 Kings 19:35; Isa. 37:36). In a vision the prophet Zechariah saw the Angel of the Lord, who appeared as a man standing among myrtle trees and who communicated with Zechariah (Zech. 1:8–17). This angel also admonished Joshua the high priest, whom Zechariah saw in a vision (3:1–10).

The Identification of the Angel of God

Who is this angel who is called God and who ministered to people by giving them directions and giving prophecies that were later fulfilled? No other angel was capable of making predictions.

Two views regarding this angel's identification have been set forth. Some say the angel of the Lord is another creature-angel with special credentials, a special place among the holy angels, and a special relationship to God. The other view identifies the angel of the Lord as the preincarnate Christ. In other words, He is the second person of the

Godhead, the eternal Son of God, appearing before He was born to Mary.[1] David wrote that the Angel of the Lord troubles those who dishonor God (Ps. 35:5–6).

The evidence seems to support overwhelmingly the latter view—the angel of the Lord was none other than the preincarnate Son of God. If this can be established, it means that centuries before Jesus was born in Bethlehem, He walked on earth, manifesting Himself as a ministering angel. True, the New Testament nowhere states that Jesus of Nazareth was the Angel of the Lord of Old Testament times. Yet many things point to that conclusion.

Christ Is the Eternal Son of God

Christ has existed eternally as the Son of God.[2] Though no specific verse states this truth precisely that way, the evidence pointing in that direction is overwhelming. Whenever the title is used of Him, it speaks of His divine essence. His fierce critics, the Jewish religious leaders, did not fail to make the connection between His repeated claims that God is His Father and His claim for deity, that He is equal with God the Father (John 5:18; 10:30–48; 20:28–31).

When the title "Son of God" is used of Christ, it has nothing to do with His birth to Mary. As the Son of God, He was not born; He was given. That is precisely what the prophet Isaiah said of Him. "For a child will be born to us, a son will be *given* to us" (Isa. 9:6, italics added). The term "Son of God" refers to Christ's eternal relationship to the Father. He was born as a child (Greek, *teknon*, "child," means one born of parents), to Mary. But the Greek word *huios* ("son") refers to an heir destined to receive an inheritance.

At the time of creation the Son of God already existed. In fact, He had a vital part in it (Col. 1:16–17; Heb. 1:2).

Christ, the Son of God, is described as being in the Father's bosom (John 1:18; 1 John 1:1–3). Thus the Son of God is as eternal as God the Father. Also the fact that God the Father sent the Son into the world (Isa. 9:6; John 3:16; 10:21; Rom. 8:32; Gal. 4:4; 1 John 4:10, 14) points to Jesus' preexistence.

The terms *firstborn* and *only begotten* describe Christ's eternal relationship to the Father. "Firstborn" speaks of Christ's priority, preeminence, dignity, rank, and position as the Son of God, and "only begotten" describes Christ's uniqueness. He is the only-one-of-a-kind Son of God.

John F. Walvoord gives an excellent summary of the biblical teaching on Christ's eternal sonship. "The scriptural view of the Sonship of Christ as recognized in many of the great creeds of the church is that Christ was always the Son of God by eternal generation and that He took upon Himself humanity through generation of the Holy Spirit; the human birth was not in order to become a Son of God but because He was the Son of God."[3]

Therefore, since He existed from eternity, it should be no surprise that Christ appeared in the Old Testament.

The Angel of the Lord Is Called God

In his first recorded appearance on earth the angel of the Lord is identified as God. After He spoke to Hagar, Abraham's runaway slave girl, He is identified as God (Gen. 16:13). The same was true later when Abraham was about to kill his son in obedience to God (22:15–16). Also Jacob used "God" and "the angel" interchangeably (48:15–16). Sometimes the words "the angel of God" are used instead of "the angel of the LORD" (Gen. 21:17; 31:11; Exod. 14:19; Judg. 13:9). Both of these are names for God and thus ascribe deity to the angel. ("*The* angel of God" should not be confused with "*an* angel of God," which could refer to any unnamed angel.)

The Angel of the Lord Is Distinct from Yahweh

The prophet Zechariah received a number of visions from God. In one of them the angel of the Lord actually addressed the Lord (Zech. 1:12–13). The two therefore could not be the same person since they spoke to each other. Yet this would indicate that the angel of the Lord is a member of the Trinity. The same prophet also wrote that the angel of the Lord and the Lord differ (3:1–2). Though both are fully divine, the two are not the same person.

The Angel of the Lord Is Christ, the Second Person of the Trinity

The evidence presented this far shows that "the angel of the Lord" is Christ. We saw that Christ has existed in eternity past as the Son of God. Then it was established that the Angel of the Lord is called Lord and God. Also this angel is distinct from Yahweh, the first person of the Trinity.

Besides these observations, four lines of evidence show that the Angel of the Lord is the second person of the Trinity in His preincarnate state. First, the visible member of the Godhead in the New Testament is Christ, the Son of God. Second, "the angel of the Lord" does not appear after the incarnation of Christ. Third, the ministries of Christ and the Angel of the Lord match. Both were sent by God the Father to minister on earth for Him. Fourth, the Angel of the Lord could not be the first person of the Trinity because no one can look on God and live. Yet Christ was certainly visible while here on earth. The Father is also the One who sent the Son. The third person of the Trinity, the Holy Spirit, was not visible either. True, He did appear at Christ's baptism as a dove, but the dove, not the Holy Spirit, was seen.[4]

Also the ministries of Christ while on earth and the ministries of the Angel of the Lord parallel each other. Dickason lists several parallel ministries. Both Christ and the Angel of the Lord were engaged in revelation, commission, deliverance, protection, intercession, advocacy, confirmation of God's covenant, comfort, and judgment.[5]

We may therefore conclude that Christ, the Son of the Living God, was the angel of the Lord of Old Testament times. His appearances are called theophanies, appearances of God, or more accurately Christophanies, appearances of Christ.

Satan, also called Lucifer

"Even Satan disguises himself as an angel of light." (2 Corinthians 11:14)

CHAPTER SIX
The Angel Called Satan

———❦———

"T HE DEVIL MADE ME DO IT" has been one of many attention-getting bumper stickers. This message is no doubt intended to get the viewer to think he or she can get off the hook, so to speak, because whatever is done that violates God's or man's laws is caused by the devil. Then, too, the message implies the devil or Satan is real. Satan is not a mere figure of speech or a mythical concept of evil. He could not be if, in fact, he is the cause of all the evil in the world.

Is Satan called an angel in the Bible? Yes, the apostle Paul referred to him as "an angel of light" (2 Cor. 11:14). Some of the Corinthian Christians were being deceived, just like Eve had been deceived by the serpent in the Garden of Eden. The serpent or Satan used craft to deceive her, and he was doing the same thing to the Corinthians. How was he doing this? They were being led astray by those who preached a different Jesus and therefore a different gospel. Those proclaiming the false message to the Corinthians were deceitful, disguising themselves as Christ's apostles, which they were not. Satan, whom the false teachers served, did the same thing, Paul said. When Satan's servants do it, it is therefore not surprising.

SATAN IS FOR REAL

Where did Satan come from? Did he always exist? If so, was he always evil? If he did not always exist, did God create him? These and related questions have often been asked. The Bible does provide answers which we must by faith accept, even though they may raise additional questions that are not answered.

The Bible is full of references to Satan. He is also called by a large number of other names. He is referred to in seven books of the Old Testament. Every writer of the New Testament wrote of him. In the Gospels, Satan is mentioned twenty-nine times, and in twenty-five of these Christ was speaking. Early in the Bible and in human history Satan appeared, and he did so without explanation. Our first parents were there in the Garden and suddenly Satan appeared on the scene. Where did he come from? How did he ever get into that place of beauty and bliss?

First, we must acknowledge that God, as we have seen earlier, created all the angels. And since He is God, He created them holy and sinless. The angels must be included in God's assessment of His creative work of creation week when He said, "It was very good" (Gen. 1:31). This is true of angels, whether they were created before or after God created the people and things mentioned in Genesis.

Satan is therefore a fallen creature. But there was a time when he was not. God brought him and all the other angels into existence in a state of creature perfection. Satan must never be viewed as God's equal, vying with God for control of the world. God and Satan are not similar to the good side and the dark side of the "force" portrayed in *Star Wars*. Such a dualistic concept is foreign to God's Word. God and Satan are not in a cosmic struggle to gain control of the world, for God alone is in control and sovereign. Satan is like a dog on his master's leash. He cannot do anything anywhere, anytime, to anybody, without God's permission. Yes, he is God's enemy and ours, but he is an enemy who must obey God even though he hates Him.

Contrary to the thinking of some, Satan and the devil are not merely names for evil powers and bad things that happen in the world. Satan is just as much a person as God is. He possesses the essential traits or characteristics of personality—intellect, emotion, and will. The devil's ability to scheme by means of deception argues for his ability to think or exercise his intellect. He did this with Eve and is still doing it (2 Cor. 11:3). The fact that he can communicate with others as he did with Jesus (Luke 4:1–12) lends further support to the fact that he possesses personality.

Satan's evil desires led him to oppose God and His plan (Isa. 14:12–17). This activity involved emotions, to be sure. The same is true of Satan's temptation of Christ and his continued temptation of people ever since. All the evil work of Satan reveals his evil will to carry out his opposition to God. An evil power or influence does not carry out a determined plan to defeat and destroy; personality is required to do this.

Personal pronouns are used of Satan throughout the Bible. The devil is often presented, and his evil plans described in association with other persons. As a moral intelligence Satan is responsible for his actions, and therefore he will be judged by God for his actions.

Satan appeared to our first parents in a deceptive way. He came to them as the serpent and tempted them to eat of the fruit God had forbidden them to eat. The serpent in Genesis 3 is clearly identified with Satan in Revelation 12:9: "The serpent of old who is called the devil and Satan," and in Revelation 20:2: "The serpent of old, who is the devil and Satan." Satan used the serpent as his instrument to get the first woman and man to rebel against God. But when did Satan sin? And how did he fall from the state of perfection in which God created him?

SATAN'S ORIGINAL SIN

All who take the Bible seriously agree that Satan is presented there as the wicked one. No one knows for sure, however, when he sinned or even if Scripture anywhere gives us a record of his fall. Two major passages of Scripture are usually said to describe his original condition before he sinned and his sin—Ezekiel 28:11–19 and Isaiah 14:12–19. Not all agree, however, that Satan is in view in these passages.[1] If he is not, we do not have any record of his rebellion against God. That, of course, would in no way make him less wicked and less rebellious. There are good reasons to believe Satan is the subject in these two passages, though one should avoid dogmatism on the matter.

Ezekiel 28:11–19

Again the word of the LORD came to me saying, "Son of man, take up a lamentation over the king of Tyre, and say to him, 'Thus says the LORD God, "You had the seal of perfection, full of wisdom and perfect in beauty. You were in Eden, the garden of God; every precious stone was your covering: the ruby, the topaz, and the diamond; the beryl, the onyx, and the jasper; the lapis lazuli, the turquoise, and the emerald; and the gold, the workmanship of your settings and sockets, was in you. On the day that you were created they were prepared. You were the anointed cherub who covers, and I placed you there. You were on the holy mountain of God; you walked in the midst of the stones of fire. You were blameless in your ways from the day you were created, until unrighteousness was found in you. By the abundance of your trade you were internally filled with violence, and you sinned; therefore I have cast you as profane from the mountain of God. And I have destroyed you, O covering cherub, from the midst of the stones of fire. Your heart was lifted up because of your beauty; you corrupted your wisdom by reason of your splendor. I cast you to the ground; I put you before kings, that they may see you. By the multitude of your iniquities, in the unrighteousness of your trade, you profaned your sanctuaries. Therefore I have brought fire from the midst of you; it has consumed you, and I have turned you to ashes on the earth in the eyes of all who see you. All who know you among the peoples are appalled at you; You have become terrified, and you will be no more." ' "

Ezekiel prophesied in the sixth century B.C. He grew up in Jerusalem and lived there until he, along with many other Jews, was taken captive by Nebuchadnezzar to Babylon. There he had relative freedom and prophesied over a period of twenty-two years. Ezekiel's primary ministry was to the Jewish exiles in Babylonia.

God called Ezekiel to keep before the exiles the sins that caused them to be there. Along with that he also encouraged them by reminding them of God's faithfulness to the promises He made to them in His covenants. The first twenty-four chapters of the Book of Ezekiel were written before Jerusalem fell to the Babylonians. Chapters 25 through 32 contain prophecies against a number of foreign nations. Israel's restoration to power and prominence is described in chapters 33–39. And prophecies of the coming millennial glory for Israel conclude the book in chapters 40–48.

In the section on the coming judgment on Gentile nations, Ezekiel predicted the fall of "the leader of Tyre" (28:2) or "the prince of Tyre" (KJV). There is little doubt that verses 2–10 refer to the historic figure Ethbaal III, who was at the time the ruler over the Phoenician seacoast city of Tyre. He was a very proud man, boastful of his many achievements. Ezekiel denounced him for his sinful pride and predicted his coming destruction and disgrace. But behind the human leader is Satan, the superhuman leader.

Interestingly, in verse 12 Ezekiel introduced one whom he called "the king of Tyre." This king is not the same person as "the leader of Tyre" in verse 2, because, for one thing, Ezekiel made some unusual statements about this "king": "You had the seal of perfection"; you were "full of wisdom and perfect in beauty"; "You were in Eden, the garden of God"; "You were blameless" (28:12–13, 15).

The person in verses 2–10 is called a man (vv. 2, 9), but the one in verses 11–19 is "the anointed cherub" and the "covering cherub" (vv. 14, 16). Also twice Ezekiel said this one was "created" (28:13, 15). The superlative language in verses 12 and 15—"perfect" and "blameless"—fits Satan in his prefallen state far better than it does any human leader.

Before his fall Satan had great privileges. He was indeed the greatest of all God's creatures. As noted earlier, the cherubim are a special class of angelic beings, who serve as guardians of God's holiness (Gen. 3:24).

In his vision of God Ezekiel saw "four living beings" (Ezek. 1:5), whom he later identified as cherubim (10:5, 9). If this cherub in 28:14, 16 is a description of Satan before his fall, it would mean he served, along with other angels, as a protector or honor guard of God's presence and holiness.

This cherub Ezekiel called "the king of Tyre" was at one time "in Eden, the garden of God" (28:12–13). "The holy mountain of God" seems to refer to the very presence of God from which Satan was "cast" (28:14). This casting out represents God's judgment on Satan because of his sin: "unrighteousness was found in you," "you were internally filled with violence," "you sinned," "your heart was lifted up because of your beauty," "you corrupted your wisdom by reason of your splendor," "the multitude of your iniquities," your "unrighteousness" (28:15–18). At the time of his sin he was barred from his former position in God's government, though he still has access to God to accuse His people (e.g., Job 1:6, 9; 2:1, 7; Rev. 12:10). In the middle of the coming Great Tribulation he will be restricted to earth to continue his evil work (12:7–13).

When Christ reigns on David's throne in Jerusalem over the whole world in the millennial kingdom, Satan will be confined to the abyss (20:1–3). At the end of this thousand-year reign of perfect peace and righteousness on earth, Satan will be loosed for a short time. Then he will be cast into the lake of fire prepared for him, where he will exist in torment forever (20:10).

Ezekiel 28:11–19, then, gives us a description of Satan's prefallen state and of his fall. Much in the passage simply cannot be applied to a mere human figure. The historic human figure is in verses 2–10, and the super-human Satan is in verses 11–19.

Isaiah 14:12–19

How have you fallen from heaven, O star of the morning, son of the dawn! You have been cut down to the earth, you who have weakened the nations! But you said in your heart, "I will ascend to heaven; I will raise my throne above the stars of God, and I will sit on the mount of assembly in the recesses of the north. I will ascend above the heights of the clouds; I will make myself like the Most High." Nevertheless you will be thrust down to Sheol, to the recesses of the pit. Those who see you will gaze at you, they will ponder over you, saying, "Is this the man who made the earth tremble, who shook kingdoms, who made the world like a wilderness and overthrew its cities, who did not allow his prisoners to go home?" All the kings of the nations lie in glory, each in his own tomb. But you have been cast out of your tomb like a rejected branch, clothed with the slain who are pierced with a sword, who go down to the stones of the pit, like a trampled corpse.

Isaiah wrote his book of prophecy in the eighth century before Christ. The enemy of God and His people at the time were Assyrian rulers. The prophet must have feared that tiny Judah would be gobbled up by Assyria.

But God miraculously intervened and did not let that happen (Isa. 36–37). Gradually Babylon gained power over Assyria, and Isaiah rightly predicted that Babylon would be used of God to punish His people for their persistent rebellion.

In his own time and way, Isaiah predicted God would also bring judgment on Babylon. And of course this did indeed happen. Through His prophet God said Israel would still exist, even after those who would conquer Babylon had been overthrown (14:1–3). There follows in chapter 14 what is called a "taunt song" deriding Babylon, the enemy of Israel and her king. We know this because Isaiah referred to Babylon by name twice in this chapter (14:4, 22).

All agree that the historic king of Babylon is in view in 14:1–11 as named in verse 4. There is disagreement, however, over whether the "star of the morning" discussed in verses 12–19 is the same as the king in verses 4–11.

Some say this entire passage (14:4–19) applies to the king of Babylon. This king was later seen as a type of Antichrist, who in the Great Tribulation will set himself "above every so-called god or object of worship . . . displaying himself as being God" (2 Thess. 2:4). Others say Isaiah spoke only of the pride and downfall of the king of Babylon,[2] a "man" "who made the earth tremble," "overthrew its cities," took many people prisoner, and yet did not even have a decent burial (Isa. 14:16–20), for he was "thrust down to Sheol" (14:15). Still others suggest that 14:12–15 is a song metaphorically portraying the city of Babylon as a god.[3] And some say the passage speaks of both the human king and Satan, who energized the king.[4]

The "star of the morning" (literally, "the shining one," 14:12)[5] seems to refer to Satan; verses 12–14 describe his sins and verses 15–19 speak of his downfall. Many think Jesus was giving a similar statement about Satan's fall in Luke 10. The seventy who had been sent out in pairs to declare "the kingdom of heaven is at hand" and to perform miracles demonstrating their authenticity returned and told Jesus that even the demons were subject to them (10:17). Jesus responded by saying, "I was watching Satan fall from heaven like lightning" (10:18). We cannot be certain Jesus was referring to Satan's fall and expulsion; perhaps He simply had in mind the fact that Satan's power was broken by Jesus' presence and message, evidenced by the victories reported by the seventy.

Five times in Isaiah 14:13–14 this "morning star" said "I will." These five statements express prideful desires that seem more fitting of Satan than of a human Babylonian king. Presumably only Satan would aspire to a position "above the stars of God" (14:13) and would seek to be "like the Most High" (14:14).

These five "I will" statements reveal Satan's sin of pride. First, he desired to be equal to God: "I will ascend to heaven." If Satan was the chief cherub of Ezekiel 28:14, 16, then he already had access to God's presence. The "I will" here must therefore refer to more than that—not just to be in God's presence, but to be equal with Him in every way.

Second, Satan asserted, "I will raise my throne above the stars of God" (Isa. 14:13). This expresses his desire to be superior over the "stars," likely a reference to all other angels. Being second in command over the angels was no longer good enough. He wanted to be the sole ruler.

Third, pride was shown by his desire to "sit on the mount of assembly in the recesses of the north" (14:13). The mountain of assembly may refer to Zion, sometimes called the mountain of God (i.e., Jerusalem), from which the Lord will reign over the earth (Ps. 48:2; Isa. 2:2–3). This then would point to Satan's desire to rule as sovereign in place of God. Some who believe the entire passage of Isaiah 14:3–21 refers to the human king of Babylon named in verse 4 say the strange language in verses 12–17 alludes to Canaanite Ugaritic mythology. For example, in 14:13 "the recesses of the north" (better, "the utmost heights of the sacred mountains," NIV) may refer to Mount Zaphon in present-day Syria, which the Canaanites said was the meeting place of their gods.

Fourth, to "ascend above the heights of the clouds" (14:14) suggests Satan's craving to acquire the glory due only to God, for only God rules above the clouds (Pss. 68:4 [He "rides on the clouds," NIV]; 104:3; Isa. 19:1; Rev. 14:14–16).

Fifth, Satan aspired to make himself "like the Most High" (Isa. 14:14). This expression speaks of obstinate defiance to God. "The Most High" describes God as Possessor of all of heaven and earth (Gen. 14:18–19). This wish of Satan was nothing short of a desire to replace God, to usurp His power and authority over all.

No one knows for certain when Satan committed this awful sin of arrogance, which sealed his eternal doom. We do know he and other angels sinned before our first parents sinned (Gen. 3), because Satan was there using the serpent in the garden to tempt them to sin.[6] When Satan sinned, he was "fallen from heaven" and "cut down to the earth" (Isa. 14:12). The "star of the morning, the son of the dawn," became Satan the deceiver. He "weakened the nations," "made the earth tremble," "shook kingdoms," and "made the world like a wilderness" (14:12, 16–17). In the future Satan will be "thrust down to Sheol" (14:15; also see Rev. 20:3), and ultimately his eternal destiny will be in the lake of fire (20:10).

SATAN'S NAMES

Names were important in Bible times for they were character-revealing. This is true of the names ascribed to God, humans, and both good and evil angels. Satan's names are descriptive of his person and work. Here are nine of the many names used of him in Scripture.

Satan

Satan is the name most often used for the archenemy of God and humans. In Hebrew the word for Satan means "adversary." This is his true character. One of the early references to the master of deception in his role of opposition to God was when he moved David to number the Israelites (1 Chron. 21:1). Elsewhere the Old Testament mentions Satan seventeen other times and only in Job 1:6–9, 12; 2:1–4, 6–7 and Zechariah 3:1–2. The New Testament mentions Satan thirty-four times in twelve books.

The Devil

"Devil" is the second most common name for the head of the fallen angels. It occurs in the New Testament thirty-six times. It describes his character, just as "Satan" does. The name "devil" translates the Greek *diabolos*, from a verb meaning "to throw." It is clear from this that the devil hurls accusations; he slanders, tears down, or defames God to man and man to God.

When Peter warned his readers about Satan, he called him their "adversary" and the "devil" (1 Pet. 5:8), who prowls like a lion to devour God's people. What was true of the scattered persecuted saints to whom Peter wrote is equally true for God's people today.

The Serpent

In Satan's temptation of Adam and Eve in the Garden, he used a serpent (Gen. 3:1–6). The apostle Paul wrote to the Corinthian Christians that Eve's downfall resulted from the serpent's craftiness (2 Cor. 11:3). The name "serpent" describes his subtlety and beguiling nature. The apostle John identified the serpent in Genesis 3:7–9 with the devil, Satan, and the "great dragon" (Rev. 12:9). Like a subtle snake or a destructive dragon, he wants to devastate God and His people.

Beelzebul

The Pharisees used this name to describe the ruler of the demons or Satan when they tried to explain how Jesus cast out demons (Matt. 12:24; also see 9:34; 10:25). They could not deny what Jesus was doing, so they said He was doing His work in the power of Beelzebul. This name perhaps derives from Baal-Zebub, god of the Philistine city of Ekron (2 Kings 1:2). "Beel-Zebub" means "lord of the flies," and Beelzebul comes from a Hebrew construction meaning "lord of filth." These two words, then, are suggestive of flies swarming over the trash heap outside the city of Jerusalem. To say Jesus' power was demonic and was by means of the lord of filth or the lord of flies was so despicable that it amounted to blasphemy of the Holy Spirit (Matt. 12:31). Their view, Jesus said, would mean that in casting out demons He was working against Himself (12:25–26).

Ruler, Prince

When Satan fell because of his sin, he instituted a counter-kingdom. He rules the *cosmos*, the world or orderly system of wicked angels and unregenerate humans.

This counter-kingdom over which Satan rules is the opposite of and stands in defiance of God's rule. Three times Jesus used this name for Satan, calling him "the ruler of this world" (John 12:31; 14:30; 16:11).

The apostle Paul called Satan a "prince" as he described the Ephesian Christians' hopeless condition before they came to faith in Christ. They "formerly walked according to the course of this world, according to the prince of the power of the air" (Eph. 2:2). In the same sentence Paul referred to Satan as "the spirit that is now working in the sons of disobedience." Though those outside of Christ may not be aware of it, Satan is at work in their minds and emotions, seeking to keep them from trusting Christ. This parallels the spiritual blindness Paul referred to when he wrote to the Corinthian Christians (2 Cor. 4:4). Though Satan is the ruler or prince of the world system that opposes God, his empire or rule is limited. He is not sovereign as God is. All Satan does is under the wise permission of God Himself and for His own good purposes.

The God of This World

As "the god of this world," Satan heads up an anti-God philosophy that permeates the thinking of the unsaved. The Greek word translated "world" in 2 Corinthians 4:4 (in Satan's title "the god of this world") is not the usual term for world (*cosmos*); it is *aion*, "age." The same word *aion* appears in Galatians 1:4, which refers to "this present evil age."

Satan "has blinded the minds of the unbelieving, that they might not see the light of the gospel of the glory of Christ" (2 Cor. 4:4). This means all unbelievers are supernaturally blinded to their need of Christ and His power to redeem. Only the supernatural power of the Holy Spirit can remove that blindness. He does just that through the Word which we are to proclaim (4:2–5).

As God's ambassadors we have the privilege and responsibility of sharing the good news of God's saving grace in Christ. We must remember though that we cannot convict sinners of their need of Christ; neither can we redeem them. The Holy Spirit alone convicts of sin, draws the sinner, shows the unsaved his or her need of Christ, and enables the sinner to believe.

The Tempter

Matthew named Satan "the tempter" when Satan confronted Jesus in the wilderness (Matt. 4:3). Our Lord was led there by the Holy Spirit of God to be "tempted by the devil" (4:1). In chapter 8 I discuss this assault against the sinless Son of God by Satan himself.

Also the apostle Paul referred to Satan as "the tempter" (1 Thess. 3:5). This name describes his work that began after his own fall and will continue until he is cast into the lake of fire. This name highlights one of Satan's major activities—tempting others to sin.

The Dragon

Webster's Dictionary defines a dragon as "a huge serpent" or "a fabulous animal generally represented as a monstrous winged and scaly serpent or saurian with a crested head and enormous claws."[7] To call Satan a dragon suggests his power and strength and the vast devastation he is capable of causing. John saw Satan as a red dragon with seven heads and ten horns, who with the demons of hell were arrayed against the Lord and His people (Rev. 12:3–4, 7, 9, 13, 16–17).

In addition, as a dragon Satan in the Great Tribulation will empower the Antichrist and people will worship the dragon (13:1–4). He is also called the dragon in 16:13 and 20:2.

The Evil One

In calling Satan "the evil one" Jesus and John both depicted him as totally corrupt and carrying on a corrupt and evil work (John 17:15; 1 John 5:18–19). Evil beyond description, Satan personally seeks to influence the whole world toward wickedness, just as he did with Cain (1 John 3:12). Kenneth Wuest suggests that the last part of 1 John 5:19 may be rendered, "the whole world in the Pernicious One is lying."[8] That is, Satan holds in his lap the whole world. But believers, John affirmed, are exempt from this awful grip of Satan (5:18). This evil one, John wrote, can be overcome by the Word of God (2:13–14).

These many names of Satan describe his evil nature and intent, and his awesome power. He is the believer's supernatural enemy. What is more, as we will see in chapter 7, Satan has a host of wicked angels at his command to assist him in his battle against God and His people.

SATAN, THE SERPENT, IN EDEN

Satanic activity on the earth has always been evil. His opposition to God on planet earth began in the Garden of Eden. Here God the Creator placed the first human pair in a perfect environment, a place of pleasure and delight. We do not know for sure where the Garden of Eden was located, but a likely probability is the highlands of Armenia near the Tigris and Euphrates rivers in what is today southeastern Turkey.

Adam and Eve had the privilege of cultivating and keeping the Garden (Gen. 2:15), and they could eat the fruit from all the trees except one (2:16–17). The tree of the knowledge of good and evil was off limits. God told our first parents that if they ate of that tree, they would die (2:17). We do not know what kind of fruit the forbidden tree bore, and it does not matter. Adam and Eve knew which tree it was and what would happen if they ate that fruit.

This time of testing, the probation period, may have been short or long. We do not know. The same is true of a similar period for the holy angels. A large company of other angels followed Satan in his rebellion against God. Each one sinned individually. Since angels do not reproduce after their kind, their sin was not passed on to any posterity. In the case of the first humans, however, their sin affected all who would be born after them (Rom. 5:12). In other words, their sin was passed on to their children and theirs to their children, and so it goes on until the end of time.

To carry out his evil work Satan used the beautiful and crafty serpent (Gen. 3:1; Rev. 12:9). Eve was familiar with the serpent and no doubt had no fear of it. Before God's curse came on the serpent, it may very well have been the most beautiful of all the creatures except man. The serpent was not originally a writhing reptile out to kill. The curse brought all that about.

The approach Satan used with Eve to get her to eat the forbidden fruit is the same approach he uses today. Times change, conditions change, kinds of sin vary, but Satan's methods remain the same. First, of course, he used the serpent with whom Eve was familiar and whom she trusted. Second, Satan raised doubt in her mind as to exactly why God placed one prohibition on her and Adam (Gen. 3:1–3). The devil really wanted Eve to deny God's right to do such a thing if He truly loved her. But before that he got Eve to doubt God's word.

Third, before long, Satan reversed what God had said and denied God's word. In other words, Satan was saying God had lied to Eve and Adam (3:4). Eve had already added to what God had said to her (3:3).

Fourth, after creating doubt in Eve's mind about the goodness, love, and justice of God and saying that God was lying, Satan proposed to tell her the "real truth" about the forbidden fruit: If she ate what God told her not to eat, she could become like God, "knowing good and evil" (3:5). All she and Adam needed to do was act independently of God. That, it must be remembered, is exactly what Satan did when he sinned before the creation of man (Isa. 14:13–14). He too exercised independence of God and His plan for him.

Throughout Scripture Satan is active, carrying out his nefarious work opposing God. Early on he seems to have concentrated on seeking to do everything in his power to keep the promise of the Seed of the woman, Christ, from being born and bruising his head, which represents a mortal wound (Gen. 3:15). Also, he continually seeks to get individuals to act independently of God just as he himself did and as he succeeded in getting Eve and Adam to do. As we shall see in chapter 8, Satan, the great enemy of our souls, is still using his crafty schemes to oppose God and His people (2 Cor. 2:11).

SATAN'S SNARES

A snare is "something by which one is entangled, involved in difficulties, held fast, or impeded . . . something deceptively attractive."[9] This description fits Satan perfectly. When we know the biblical picture of him, we are better prepared to avoid his snares.

Knowing Satan and His Methods

Being aware of Satan's tactics can help believers lead victorious Christian lives. Even his titles, as discussed in this chapter, tell much about his wicked nature and work. Several passages of Scripture discuss the tactics Satan uses to trip up God's children—to get them to sin, to catch them in his snare.

In 2 Corinthians 2:11 Paul alerted the Corinthian Christians about Satan's subtle schemes or devices. The apostle urged them to forgive and restore an erring brother who had been disciplined by them, "in order that no advantage be taken of us by Satan; for we are not ignorant of his schemes." Satan operates according to a planned strategy and every believer needs to understand that and act accordingly.

Paul told the Ephesian Christians to "put on the full armor of God, that you may be able to stand firm against the schemes of the devil" (Eph. 6:11). The apostle John wrote of Satan as the great deceiver, "who deceives the whole world" (Rev. 12:9).

Peter exhorted believers to "be on the alert" because the devil "prowls about like a roaring lion seeking someone to devour" (1 Pet. 5:8). Always deceptive, Satan masquerades as someone or something other than he really is (2 Cor. 11:14). His true colors are seldom visible as he engages in his nefarious work.

Peter said the way believers are to respond to Satan is to "resist" him while being firm in faith (1 Pet. 5:9). Before the terse description of the devil's maneuvers the saints were told, "Humble yourselves, therefore, under the mighty hand of God" (5:6) and cast "all your anxiety upon Him" (5:7). These Christian graces enable believers to be successful in resisting Satan.

Knowing Ourselves and Our Weaknesses

Everyone is born with a built-in capacity for and tendency to sin. We call this the sin nature. Received from our parents and passed on to our children, this sin nature is not removed at the time of salvation. Of course, when a person is saved, he or she receives a new nature, a new capacity and tendency to obey God. But the old sin nature remains. In the power

ANGELS, SATAN, AND DEMONS

of the indwelling Holy Spirit God's children can have victory over sin as they yield to Him and live according to Scripture.

Knowing our spiritual weaknesses and the potential for evil in us is absolutely essential if we are to avoid the snares of Satan. The apostle Paul said he knew "that nothing good dwells in me, that is, in my flesh [the sin nature]; for the wishing is present in me, but the doing of the good is not" (Rom. 7:18).

We will never be prepared to avoid the snares of Satan unless and until we acknowledge our captivity and inner desire to sin. And of course Satan knows all our weak points and always attacks where he knows he can gain the best foothold.

Knowing and Appropriating God's Provision

A third way to avoid Satan's snares is to know and appropriate God's bountiful provisions, all of which have been made available through Jesus Christ's work on the cross.

Discussed in chapter 8, these include the commands to "be filled with the Spirit" (Eph. 5:18) and to "walk by the Spirit" (Gal. 5:16). Additional provisions by which Christians can offset the attacks of Satan, their archenemy, include the work of God the Son, the work of God the Holy Spirit, and the written Word of God.

To know about these great divine provisions from God is helpful, but it is not enough. We must also appropriate them at specific times throughout our Christian pilgrimage. We are responsible to surrender to Him, His Son, His Spirit, and His holy Word.

How wonderful to know God has not only provided salvation for us; He has also given all we need for life and godliness (2 Pet. 1:3). We should continually pray, "God, give me the courage and conviction to carry out what you have assigned to me for victory."

Common Snares of Satan

Some of the snares or deceptive schemes by which Satan seeks to trap believers are worry, the world, and work.

The snare of worry. We live in fretful and frightful times. Each day seems to bring more and more pressure on us. Some of this we bring on ourselves, whereas some is simply unavoidable.

In His Sermon on the Mount Jesus made a point of telling His own, "Do not be anxious for your life" (Matt. 6:25). Reminding them of the birds and the lilies of the field which He cares for, He assured them He would care for them since they are far more important to Him than birds and flowers (6:26–31).

Peter exhorted his Christian readers to cast all their anxiety on the Lord because He cares for them (1 Pet. 5:7). All of us must learn to experience rest in Him no matter how great the pressures. "Do not fret yourself because of evildoers" (Prov. 24:19).

Satan enjoys it when we get ourselves upset and agitated by worrying. Someone has well remarked that most of what we worry about never comes to pass. One of the devil's tricks is to keep us so busy worrying about things we can do nothing about that we fail to do anything about the things we can change.

The snare of the world. The apostle John exhorted us, "Do not love the world" (1 John 2:15). The "world," as Charles Ryrie explains, is "that system organized by Satan, headed by Satan, and run by Satan, which leaves God out and is a rival to Him."[10] That is an accurate definition of the *cosmos* or world which we are not to love. John even went a little further in his command to believers. Not only are they not to love the world; they also are not to love "the things in the world" (2:16).

The "world" refers not to the earth or people on it (as it is used elsewhere in Scripture). The "world" is Satan's highly organized anti-God system, of which he is "the ruler" (John 12:31). Anything and everything that promotes that system and advances Satan's cause is not to be loved by God's people. The satanic system utilizes things we see, read, listen to, and do. These are avenues Satan uses to promote his godless cause. We must always be on guard lest he snare us by worldliness.

The snare of work. Some Christians are lazy, whereas others are workaholics. Both laziness and unrelenting work can be snares used by Satan. The idle mind, as the saying goes, is the devil's workshop. The materialistic age in which we live makes its mark on Christians and non-Christians alike. "Keeping up with the Joneses" is what many unbelievers try to do, and unfortunately Christians often engage in the same frantic pursuit of material things.

Often Satan gets God's people so busy doing things, many of which are not bad in themselves, that the more important things are often left undone. The devil is not omniscient, but he knows where he can set his snares to trap us. His major goal is to keep us from being successful in our Christian lives, and he seeks to do whatever he can to accomplish this. Sometimes he may seek to keep us so busy serving the Lord that we do not take time to worship Him. Or he may try to keep us discouraged, depressed, defeated.

Satan uses many other snares as well. The three mentioned above serve to illustrate the point. Satan, our enemy, is bent on our destruction. Apart from God's help, we would be devoured by him (1 Pet. 5:8). In God's strength, however, we can resist him (5:9) and "stand firm" against him (Eph. 6:11). As discussed elsewhere in this book, Satan is a defeated foe. The Lord Jesus Christ defeated him at Calvary. Proof of that is the open tomb. Christ arose triumphantly over Satan and death. The finished work of Christ is our source of victory over every snare of Satan. Therefore we need to claim victory by faith.

Christ's Temptation

"Then Jesus said to him, 'Begone, Satan! For it is written, "You shall worship the Lord your God, and serve Him Only."' Then the devil left Him; and behold, angels came and began to minister to Him." (Matt. 4:10–11)

CHAPTER SEVEN
Satan's Angels

THIS STUDY, like the previous one about Satan, touches our every day Christian experience because both Satan and his angels are our enemies. Learning about our spiritual enemies helps us realize that our great God is sovereign. Neither Satan nor his myriads of helpers can do anything God does not allow them to do. We learn more about ourselves, too, as we study about demons. We are the objects of their wicked attention. If we are not walking with God, we are opening the door to our spiritual adversaries. The more we study and learn about Satan and his angels, the more we see the need to draw closer to our Lord for victory and the need to live in the power of the Spirit, since the Spirit is the divine Counterforce to the evil work of demons.

This chapter examines what the Bible teaches about wicked angels in response to four questions: Do demons really exist? Where did demons come from? How are demons described in the Bible? What can demons do?

DO DEMONS REALLY EXIST?

Many non-Christians, and even some professing Christians, believe demons exist only in our imagination. Some view demons as forces of evil but not as spirit beings with personality. Others assign them to fairy-tale and folklore mentality. This is apparently the best explanation they can come up with for all the current occult activity and literature and the evils in the world. But there are many experiences that defy human explanation.

The Bible contains many references to demons, wicked angels, and Satan's angels, with a lot of information about what they do.

Before we look at the testimony of Scripture for the reality of their existence, however, we need to be reminded that belief in these evil helpers of Satan has always been a part of heathen religions, especially of eastern nations. Merrill Unger discusses this fact:

> The history of various religions from the earliest times shows belief in Satan and demons to be universal. According to the Bible, degeneration from monotheism resulted in the blinding of men by Satan and the most degrading forms of idolatry (Romans 1:21–32; 2 Corinthians 4:4). By the time of Abraham (c. 2000 B.C.), men had sunk into a crass polytheism that swarmed with evil spirits. Spells, incantations, magical texts, exorcisms, and various forms of demonological phenomena abound in archaeological discoveries from Sumeria and Babylon. Egyptian, Assyrian, Chaldean, Greek, and Roman antiquity are rich in demonic phenomena. The deities worshiped were invisible demons represented by material idols and images.
>
> The great ethnic faiths of India, China, and Japan major in demonism, as well as the animistic religions of Africa, South America, and some islands. Even the ancient Bible lands swarmed with demons.[1]

SATAN'S ANGELS IN THE OLD TESTAMENT

The wicked angels of Satan are not always called demons in the Old Testament. Though there are only a few references to demons, the work of Satan and his helpers is evident everywhere.

The children of Israel were instructed not to offer the blood of animals that had been killed for food to "goat demons" (Lev. 17:7). These were apparently goatlike demons some people worshiped.

On the eve of his death Moses spoke words of warning, rebuke, and encouragement to the Israelite assembly (Deut. 32). In the song he spelled out details of Israel's rebellion at one point in her history. He said, "They sacrificed to demons, who were not God" (32:17). Psalm 106:37 refers to the same thing: "They even sacrificed their sons and their daughters to the demons."

Since Satan is not omnipresent, that is, everywhere present at the same time, the only way to account for all the opposition to God, deceit, and waywardness of God's people is to acknowledge that Satan's angels are assisting him.

SATAN'S ANGELS IN THE NEW TESTAMENT

Much of the New Testament teaching about demons comes from the recorded words of Christ in the synoptic Gospels.

The Savior gave His twelve disciples power over "unclean spirits" (Matt. 10:1). This description is another name for Satan's angels. It was not uncommon for Jesus Himself to cast demons out of people. Matthew tells us He healed "a demon-possessed man" (12:22). When the Pharisees heard about the incident, they could not deny the miracle He had performed, so they said He did it, as we noted in chapter 6, in the power of "Beelzebul the ruler of the demons" (12:24). Jesus rebuked them sharply and told them He cast out demons by the Spirit of God (12:28).

On one occasion when Jesus was in the district of Tyre and Sidon, a Canaanite woman who had a daughter who was demon-possessed came to Him for help. Without touching or even seeing the girl, the Lord delivered her of the demons (15:22–28).

On another occasion a man came to Jesus who had a son who was demon-possessed. He behaved like a "lunatic" (17:15). The disciples were not spiritually prepared to help the man, but Jesus rebuked the demon and he came out of the boy.

The lake of fire, Jesus said, was prepared for "the devil and his angels" (25:41). Humans who reject Christ as their Substitute for sin will go there also, but the place was intended for Satan and his angels.

The occasion when Christ allowed "unclean spirits" to indwell swine is one of the most familiar accounts of His encounter with demons. A legion of demons possessed a man from the country of the Gerasenes. When Christ cast them out of the man, the demons acknowledged His deity and begged to be cast into the swine. It was done, and the possessed man was completely restored to sanity and health (Mark 5:1–20).

The rest of the New Testament includes many references to Satan's angels. Each of the writers of the Gospels records several cases of demon possession and Christ's deliverance. We will discuss demon possession and exorcism in chapters 10 and 11. The only New Testament book that makes no mention of demons is Hebrews.

IS IT REASONABLE TO BELIEVE IN SATAN'S ANGELS?

For Bible believers, what the Old and New Testaments affirm concerning demons is all that is necessary to establish that they really do exist. Defense for the existence of demons can also be found from reason, however. How else can the presence and manifestation of all the evil in the world be explained? What about the widespread belief in evil spirits? How can this be accounted for apart from the reality of these wicked beings? Furthermore, demonic possession of and power over people is the most logical explanation of the behavior of men like Adolf Hitler, Adolf Eichmann, and contemporaries of similar behavior. It is not at all satisfying to believe that what Jim Jones did in Jonestown or David Koresh did in Waco, Texas, was simply the result of a mental disorder. Their crimes were too heinous for such an explanation. Behind and alongside such atrocities were Satan and his angels. The humans involved performed the awful deeds and for them they are personally responsible, but they were prompted and energized by the personal forces of hell.

WHERE DID DEMONS COME FROM?

When Satan fell from his holy state in which God created him, a host of other holy angels fell with him. They followed him in his rebellion against God and the place He had for them in His world. How many holy angels sinned along with Satan? Some believe a third of them did, based on Revelation 12:4, "And his [Satan's] tail swept away a third of the stars of heaven." Others understand this passage to be referring to an atmospheric phenomenon, perhaps a great meteor shower, which will be caused by Satan in the Tribulation. Still others suggest that in the Tribulation Satan will extend his power over his opponents.

The Bible does not tell us exactly when some of God's angels became Satan's angels. As mentioned earlier, the time of Satan's sin is not revealed either. That all the holy angels had a period of probation during which they were tested as to their obedience to God seems probable.

We conclude that a host of holy angels sinned when Satan did and in the same way. Here are the reasons for this belief. First, we know that wicked angels exist and we know God did not create them wicked. They sinned at some point after God created them holy. Second, we know some of Satan's angels are free to roam in the world and afflict God's people (Eph. 6:11–12). Others of them are confined and therefore restricted because they are bound in chains of darkness until the day of their judgment (2 Pet. 2:4). This fact seems to indicate that some of the angels who followed Satan in his rebellion committed an additional sin for which God bound them.

Third, the most logical time and location to place this sin of the holy angels by which they became demons or Satan's angels is when Satan himself sinned.

The testimony of Scripture is that all wicked angels are demons. These angels who sinned when Satan did became known as his angels (Matt. 25:41). They are also called demons (12:24). And both angels and demons are called "spirits" (Ps. 104:4, KJV; Matt. 8:16). Both also carry on similar activities (17:14–18; Luke 22:3; Mark 9:17; Rev. 9:13).

Many believe "the sons of God" in Genesis 6:2 were wicked angels, who have been confined in chains because of their horrendous crime. The other wicked angels who were not involved in that sin are the ones now free to roam. (See the excursus on the sons of God toward the end of this chapter.)

A totally nonbiblical view of the origin of demons is that demons are simply the products of superstition or are names for certain diseases. Another view, held especially by the ancient Greeks, is that demons are the spirits of very wicked people who have died. But there is no Scripture to support such a view. Still others believe demons are the progeny of the union of the "sons of God" with "the daughters of men" in Genesis 6. Those who believe in a pre-Adamic race hold that demons are the disembodied spirits of the pre-Adamic race. Again, no Scripture supports a pre-Adamic race, to say nothing about the leap from such a race to demons.

HOW ARE DEMONS DESCRIBED IN THE BIBLE?

Spirit Beings with Personality

Demons, just like their peers who did not sin, are supernatural spirit beings. The major difference between the two is that demons employ their supernaturalism in service to Satan, and God's angels display theirs in service to God.

Many who were demon-possessed were brought to Jesus, and "He cast out the spirits with a word" (Matt. 8:16). When the seventy who had been sent out by Christ in pairs returned, they reported their success by saying that "even the demons" were subject to them. The Lord warned them about getting their eyes off the main purpose. In His response He called the demons "spirits" (Luke 10:17, 20).

Further proof that demons have personality is seen in the fact that Jesus conversed with them on several occasions (e.g., Mark 9:25). He rebuked them, which would have been inappropriate if they were mere forces or powers. James, our Lord's half-brother, wrote that demons fear and tremble (James 2:19). Paul told Timothy demons have a belief system (1 Tim. 4:1–3). Demons embrace certain doctrines (Mark 1:27). All these facts argue strongly for the personality of demons.

It is important to remember that demons are creatures, and though they are powerful, God has imposed definite limitations on them. They are subject to Him and His sovereign purposes.

Satan's Supernatural Servants

Satan's angels, the demons free to roam, are described as "rulers . . . powers . . . world forces of this darkness . . . spiritual forces of wickedness in the heavenly places" (Eph. 6:12). Jesus said they were "unclean spirits" (Matt. 10:1; Mark 1:23) and "evil spirits" (Luke 7:21). Such descriptions speak of their moral impurity. Could it be that this accounts for the behavior of some people who are possessed and/or controlled by them? For example, the man from the country of the Gerasenes lived in a cemetery, and no one was able to subdue him (Mark 5:1–25). The false teachers described by Peter also promoted sensuality along with their demon-inspired denial of Christ's deity (2 Pet. 2:1–2, 10, 13–14, 18).

Scripture does not tell us how much Satan's angels know, but they, along with the holy angels, do possess unusual intelligence. They knew who Jesus is (Mark 1:34). On one occasion a demon announced that Jesus is "the Son of the Most High God" (5:7). Demons know, too, of God's future judgment on them (Matt. 8:29). They apparently know about God's salvation for believing sinners, because they seek to keep sinners from trusting the Savior (1 John 4:1–4). The difference between true and false doctrine is known to them, because they constantly work at corrupting sound biblical principles (1 Tim. 4:1–3).

On occasion demons in our Lord's time here on earth demonstrated great and unusual strength. Again, the maniac of Gadara illustrates this. The demons in him made him so strong that he was uncontrollable (Mark 5:1–5). Another illustration of demonic strength comes from Paul's experience at Ephesus while on his third missionary journey (Acts 19:13–16). A man possessed of demons single-handedly overpowered seven sons of a Jewish chief priest who were mocking God's power.

During the coming seven-year Great Tribulation demons will apparently control locusts, who will produce sores so painful that those who have them will seek death (Rev. 9:1–11). We can be sure these locusts will be controlled by demons because the king over them will be "the angel of the abyss," that is, Satan. His name in Hebrew is Abaddon, and in the Greek he has the name Apollyon (9:11).

A horde of demons will be released during the Great Tribulation to inspire horsemen who will ride horses with lionlike heads, with fire spewing out of their mouths, killing "a third of mankind" (9:13–19). "Spirits of demons" (16:14) in the coming campaign of Armageddon will be able to perform signs and wonders that will mimic God's miracles. The magicians in Egypt under Pharaoh did a similar thing. They, too, were no doubt energized by demons.

In summary, demons promote Satan's purposes. As his angels, they advance his cause. Just as he is engaged in hindering and counterfeiting God's work, so are they. Satan and his angels are busy all the time; they never take a break from their wicked ways.

WHAT CAN DEMONS DO?

A number of demonic activities have already been alluded to. Their general work is to promote Satan's work. They are at his command; they are like his arms and legs. This means His angels oppose God constantly. The specifics of their work may not always be the same in every age, but their allegiance to Satan remains constant.

Whether these satanic emissaries still do all the things they did in Bible times may be open to question. But presumably demons can and often do many of the same things.

An "evil spirit" was sent by God Himself to cause agitation between Abimelech, Israel's ruler, and the inhabitants of Shechem (Judg. 9:23). When the "Spirit of the LORD departed from Saul . . . an evil spirit from the LORD terrorized him" (1 Sam. 16:14). The apostle Paul was given "a messenger of Satan to torment" him to keep him humble (2 Cor. 12:7 NIV).

Demons were involved in turning people to idol worship (Lev. 17:7; Deut. 32:17). The Christians in Corinth were warned of the same danger. Gentiles, Paul said, were sacrificing to demons at the same time they thought they were sacrificing to God (1 Cor. 10:20). Demons inspire false teachers (1 John 4:1–4), and thereby they attack the very heart of Christianity—Christ's incarnation, death, resurrection, and ascension. As part of the Armageddon campaign demons will motivate military powers east of Jerusalem to cross the Euphrates River and invade Israel (Rev. 16:13–16).

During our Lord's ministry on earth demons were especially active. They inflicted various diseases on people, such as dumbness (Matt. 9:33), blindness (12:22), a form of epilepsy (17:15–18), and mental derangement (Mark 5:1–20). Do demons do these things today? The Bible does not answer this question, but it would seem that they could and probably sometimes do. However, not all physical and mental illnesses are the result of demonic activity. Even in New Testament times the two were distinct (Matt. 4:24; Luke 7:21).

Because of the reality of Satan's wickedness and his hordes of demons who carry out his bidding, believers need to walk closely to the Lord. None of us can afford to be out of fellowship with Him for even the slightest period of time. What we need to fear most is not demonic influence or oppression or even demon possession but being out of fellowship with God. As long as we walk in the light as He is in the light (1 John 1:5), live according to Scripture, and use the armor of God (Eph. 6:10–17), we have God's protection from the attacks of Satan and his angels.

God has not told us how to detect demons, how to know their names, or how to cast them out. Instead, He has exhorted us repeatedly in His Word to shun sin, make no place for Satan in our lives, and resist the devil by obeying the Lord. At the moment of salvation Jesus delivers the believing one from the power of darkness and transfers him or her into the kingdom of God's dear Son (Col. 1:14). We need to put into practice the victory Christ has already achieved for us, always keeping in mind the exalted position we have in Him. Satan is a defeated foe. Victory is ours in Christ and Him alone.

EXCURSUS
The "Sons of God" in Genesis 6

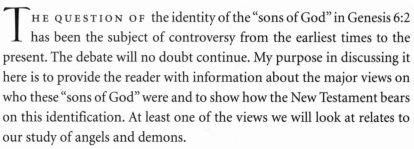

T HE QUESTION OF the identity of the "sons of God" in Genesis 6:2 has been the subject of controversy from the earliest times to the present. The debate will no doubt continue. My purpose in discussing it here is to provide the reader with information about the major views on who these "sons of God" were and to show how the New Testament bears on this identification. At least one of the views we will look at relates to our study of angels and demons.

First, we need to see the reference in its immediate context. "Now it came about, when men began to multiply on the face of the land, and daughters were born to them, that the sons of God saw that the daughters of men were beautiful; and they took wives for themselves, whomever they chose. Then the LORD said, 'My Spirit shall not strive with man forever; because he also is flesh; nevertheless his days shall be one hundred and twenty years.' The Nephilim were on the earth in those days, and also afterward, when the sons of God came in to the daughters of men, and they bore children to them. Those were the mighty men who were of old, men of renown" (Gen. 6:1–6).

Who were these "sons of God" who took the "daughters of men" to be their wives?

The identification of these "sons of God" is not of major importance to one's Christian life, but since Genesis 6 is a part of God's Word, we should certainly seek to understand it properly. A proper perspective, however, must be maintained lest we neglect other much more important things in the Bible.

The Sethite-Cainite View

In this view the "sons of God" were men from the descendants of Seth usually said to be the godly Sethites. The "daughters of men" were women from Cain's ungodly line. Their sin was that of "mixed marriages," the godly marrying the ungodly, which of course met with God's strong disapproval.

The "Sons of God" as Ambitious Despots

In this view royal leaders, perhaps demon-controlled, were "the sons of God" who took many wives to themselves, thereby as polygamists establishing royal harems. Manfred Kober defines this view in this way: "The term 'sons of God' refers to kings or nobles. The term 'sons of God' in its Near Eastern setting was a title for nobles, aristocrats, and kings. These ambitious despots lusted after power and wealth and desired to become 'men of a name' that is, somebodies (cf. 11:4)."[1] According to Allen Ross, who holds this view, Genesis 6:1–4 is a polemic against the pagan idea that kings were the offspring of gods copulating with humans.[2] Pagans thought their kings were divine, but in this view they are rightly seen as demonic. Rulers are referred to as gods in Exodus 21:6; 22:8–9, 28; and Psalm 82:6.

The "Sons of God" as Wicked Angels

In this view wicked angels who had already sinned with Satan committed another great sin. They cohabited with the "daughters of men" (Gen. 6:2) producing a strange progeny called Nephilim (6:4),[3] the consequence of which was the catastrophic Flood.

EVALUATIONS

Each of these views must address several crucial questions. (1) How does the view account for the rather unusual title "sons of God" in this context? (2) How does the view account for the Flood (which I believe was global) that followed the union of the "sons of God" with the "daughters of men"? (3) How does the view account for the strange progeny, the Nephilim or giants? (4) How does the view account for the confinement of some wicked angels in conjunction with the flood of Noah's day (2 Pet. 2:4–5; Jude 6–7)?

I believe that the view that the "sons of God" in Genesis 6:2 were wicked angels has fewer problems than the other views. Duane Garrett states his reason for holding to the wicked-angels view: "In Genesis 6:1–2 the most natural meaning to an ancient Hebrew reader would have been that supernatural beings cohabited with human women. So I presume that this is what the text means."[4]

Problems with the Sethite-Cainite View and the Ambitious Despots View

I have six problems with these views. First, there is no proof that the "daughters of men" were confined to the descendants of the Cainites. Second, elsewhere in the Old Testament the term "sons of God" always refers to angelic beings (Job 1:6; 2:1; 38:7).

Third, neither of these views explains adequately the progeny resulting from the union. How would the union of godly men and ungodly women necessarily result in their offspring being Nephilim or "men of renown"? And why would polygamists necessarily have children who became "men of renown"? Most likely, ancient writers acquired the concept of half-human and half-divine beings from some originally pure and uncorrupted source such as Genesis 6:1–4. (However, it must be admitted that scholars differ in their view of the Nephilim. Some say they were the progeny of this union of the sons of God and the daughters of men, but others say they were already on the earth before the union as well as afterward. In other words, some say the "men of renown," not the Nephilim, were the offspring.)

Fourth, if the Sethites were a "godly" line, why were they involved in marrying ungodly women?

Fifth, neither of these views satisfactorily explains Ephesians 6:12; 2 Peter 2:4; and Jude 6–7. According to these verses some demons are free to roam and afflict saints, while others are bound until the day of their judgment. The 2 Peter passage associates the bound wicked angels with Noah. In Jude 6–7 the sin causing the demons' confinement was sexual. They "did not keep their own domain but abandoned their proper abode," and they were associated with "Sodom and Gomorrah," "gross immorality," and "strange flesh." Sixth, both views must make an exception to the meaning of the phrase "sons of God" in Genesis 6:2 if it does not refer to angels.

Problems with the Wicked-Angels View

When I say I embrace the wicked-angels view, I do not mean it is free of problems. I agree there are difficulties with this view, but there may be answers to at least some of them.

First, some respond that since angels are spirit beings they could not have sex with women on the earth. Furthermore, Jesus said in Matthew 22:30 that angels are not given in marriage. However, Jesus' statement concerned holy angels, not demons. Also His statement only teaches that angels do not propagate among their own species; He did not necessarily say they could not cohabit outside their species. Further, Christ did not say angels cannot cohabit; He simply said they do not marry.

Second, some object to the wicked-angels view by noting that it seems strange for evil angels to be called "sons of God." Admittedly this is a strong objection, to which I do not have an answer (unless "sons of God" suggests the fact that they were created by Him).

Third, Matthew 24:37–39 and Luke 17:26–29 state that when Christ returns conditions on the earth will be like those in the days of Noah. But those who oppose the wicked-angels view feel it is unlikely that the sin of the "sons of God" and the "daughters of men" would be repeated. However, though neither of these passages in Matthew and Luke specifies the sin in question, it may be that the sin will be failing to prepare for coming judgment by heeding God's Word. This was the same sin as that of the "daughters of men."

We certainly cannot be dogmatic in identifying the "sons of God" in

Genesis 6. However, we can be sure that people who are sons and daughters of God through faith alone in Christ alone have commands from God to live holy lives, which includes moral purity.

EXCURSUS

The Spirits in Prison in 1 Peter 3

———— ∞∞∞ ————

F IRST PETER 3:18–20, with its reference to spirits in prison, is un-doubtedly one of the most debated passages of Scripture bearing on our study of demons. The passage reads, "For Christ also died for sins once for all, the just for the unjust, in order that He might bring us to God, having been put to death in the flesh, but made alive in the spirit; in which also He went and made proclamation to the spirits now in prison, who once were disobedient, when the patience of God kept waiting in the days of Noah, during the construction of the ark, in which a few, that is, eight persons, were brought safely through the water."

Does "made alive in the spirit" refer to Christ's human spirit or to the Holy Spirit? What is meant by "He went and made proclamation"? When was this preaching done? Who are "the spirits in prison?" What is meant by prison?

Three views are held in answer to these questions about 1 Peter 3:18–20.

The first view is that by means of the Holy Spirit Noah preached to people whose "spirits" are now in hades because they refused to believe Noah's message. This is an old view still held by many today.

E. Schuyler English stated this view this way: "The preaching was long before Saint Peter wrote, in fact in the day of Noah—preaching by the Spirit through Noah to those who were on earth in his generation, who being disobedient, were now (at the time the Apostle wrote) in prison, that is, Hades."[1] A contemporary advocate of this view described it this way: "The passage refers not to something Christ did between his death and resurrection, but to what he did 'in the spiritual realm of existence' (or 'through the Spirit') *at the time of Noah.* When Noah was building the ark, Christ 'in spirit' was preaching through Noah to the hostile unbelievers around him."[2]

There are some problems with this view. Peter wrote that the one who "made proclamation" was Christ, not Noah. Also the word "spirits," when used as it is in 1 Peter 3:19 (without a qualifying adjective) almost always refers to angels or demons, not humans. Further, this view does not harmonize with 2 Peter 2:4 and Jude 6.

A second view is that between Christ's death and resurrection He went in His human spirit to hades, where He proclaimed to all the unsaved dead that He was victorious and their doom was final.

This view, too, has some problems. It does not take "spirits" in its normal sense of angelic creatures. And the text says Christ went not to hades but to prison, which according to 2 Peter 2:4 is Tartarus, apparently a prison for some fallen angels before their ultimate doom in the eternal lake of fire. Nor does this view harmonize with 2 Peter 2:4 and Jude 6.

A third view is that between His death and resurrection, Christ went in His human spirit to Tartarus where some wicked angels are confined, and He announced (not "preached" salvation) to them His victory over death and their leader Satan and pronounced judgment on them.

The "spirits now in prison" are demons who not only sinned with Satan when he fell but who also cohabited with women of Noah's day, producing a strange progeny called Nephilim (or giants) and "men of renown." God's judgment on this sin of humans and wicked angels was the global flood of Noah's day. (See the previous excursus on the sons of God).

Kenneth W. Wuest embraced this view. "Our Lord therefore, between His death on the cross and His resurrection from Joseph's tomb, preached to the fallen angels in Tartarus."[3] More recently Alan M. Stibbs expressed the same view. "In His quickened human spirit, before His body was raised from the tomb, He was able to go where evil spirits are in prison, awaiting the judgment of the great day (2 Pet. 2:4, 5; Jude 6), and to announce to them His victory over death, and over the consequences to men of their evil-doing. He thus made them aware that their own judgment was finally sealed (cf. Col. 2:14, 15)."[4]

Several factors seem to support this view.

(1) When the term "spirits" is used in the New Testament without any defining or modifying words, it almost always refers to angels or demons, not to humans. There are some possible exceptions, however.

(2) The statement that Christ was "put to death in the flesh but made alive in the spirit" (1 Pet. 3:18) contrasts His physical body and His spirit. To make "spirit" here refer to the Holy Spirit disregards the intended contrast between Jesus' "flesh" and His "spirit." Though He died, He remained alive in His spirit.

(3) Identifying the "spirits in prison" as wicked angels harmonizes well with 2 Peter 2:4 and Jude 6. Both of these passages speak of wicked angels who are confined until their eternal judgment. Also in both passages the sin for which they are bound was sexual, which fits with Genesis 6:1–4 and our understanding of 1 Peter 3:18–20. In 2 Peter 2:4–5 Peter associated the angels who sinned in Noah's day with the sexual immorality of Sodom and Gomorrah. Jude wrote that the angels to which he referred were "kept in eternal bonds under darkness" because they "did not keep their own domain, but abandoned their proper abode" (Jude 6). If the "sons of God" in Genesis 6 and the "spirits now in prison" in 1 Peter 3:19 are not wicked angels, we have no other explanation of why some demons are bound while others are free to roam.

(4) "This view keeps the sequence of Christ's actions in order as the series of aorist [past] tenses would prefer. The order of events is 'put to death,' 'made alive in spirit,' 'went,' 'preached,' and then the resurrection and exaltation to God's right hand."[5]

(5) This view harmonizes with Peter's reference to the ultimate climax of Christ's sovereign rule "after angels and authorities and powers had been subjected to Him" (3:22).

There is a variation of this view. Some who believe the "spirits now in prison" (3:19) are demons say that in some way they were disobedient in Noah's day, possibly by influencing pagan rulers to take multiple wives. God then punished the demons by imprisoning them, and they became the bound demons of 2 Peter 2:4 and Jude 6.

Some writers hold a fourth view—that *after* Christ's resurrection and before His ascension He announced to the demons imprisoned in Tartarus His resurrection victory over them.[6]

The view I prefer is not free of problems, but it seems to have fewer problems than the other views. It also seems to harmonize well with the context of 1 Peter 3.

The Temptation of Jesus
"And he led Him up and showed Him all the kingdoms of the world in a moment of time."
(Luke 4:5)

CHAPTER EIGHT
Satan, the Savior, and the Saints of God

W HEN JESUS WAS HERE ON EARTH, did the wicked supernatural enemy of God have anything to do with Him, the Savior
of sinners? Does the enemy have anything to do with Him now? How is
the believer to do battle with Satan? How can the child of God oppose so
powerful an enemy?

In this chapter I want to give special attention to the confrontation
between Satan and the Savior and the continued conflict between Satan
and believers.

SATAN AND THE SAVIOR

The first mention of Satan in the New Testament is in the accounts of his
temptation of Jesus. As already noted, Satan and his wicked angels are far
more prominent in the New Testament than in the Old. Their concentrated attacks centered on Christ and His saving work. Long before the
Savior's birth, however, Satan did everything in his power to keep Him
from being born. After Jesus was born, Satan made repeated attempts to
disqualify and/or destroy Him as man's Redeemer. The devil's hatred of
the Son of God and his hostility and opposition to Him continued until
he was defeated at Calvary and the empty tomb.

Satan's Future Defeat (Gen. 3:15)

Just when did Satan's animosity toward the Savior begin? No specific time is stated in Scripture. It seems logical, however, to place it after his own fall and when Satan first learned of God's plan to send His Son to be man's Savior. God's promise that One would come to defeat Satan is first stated in Genesis 3:15. Evangelicals traditionally understand this prophecy to refer to the defeat of Satan by the Messiah. It has been called the *protevangelium* or the "first gospel."[1] God said to Satan: "And I will put enmity between you and the woman, and between your seed and her seed; he shall bruise you on the head, and you shall bruise him on the heel."

This is part of the divine curse on the serpent Satan used to carry out his evil work (3:14). Satan, who presented himself as wiser and more interested in Eve's welfare than God, was now cursed by the One whom he had ridiculed and put in a bad light. It is God who put enmity between the serpent and the woman, between the serpent's seed and the woman's seed, and between Satan and the woman's seed. Whatever is believed about the woman's seed and Satan's seed must harmonize with the fact that God put the "enmity" there, which makes certain the ultimate outcome.

To whom does the woman's seed refer? Some say the term simply points to her many descendants, suggesting enmity between women and snakes. But several factors indicate her seed is one person, namely, Christ. First, since the crushing blow is to come on the head of one individual (the serpent himself) and not his offspring, the implication is that a single individual is to inflict it.[2] To take the seed of the woman as collective here conflicts with the use of the singular "he" and "you." The reference is to an individual, not a group.

Second, the promise contrasts the kind of bruising to be inflicted on the serpent or Satan and the bruising to be inflicted on the woman's Seed. The one will affect the head of Satan and the other the heel (of the woman's Seed). The one suggests a mortal wound, while the other is a much less serious blow. This harmonizes well with the New Testament's teaching of Christ's defeat of Satan at the cross. The Savior did indeed suffer and die (the serpent bruised Christ's "heel"), but He arose triumphant over death, hell, and Satan (the woman's Seed bruised the serpent's "head").

Third, the Septuagint (the Greek translation of the Old Testament) in its rendering of Genesis 3:15 supports the view that "the seed" of the woman refers to an individual and is not a collective reference. Fourth, the New Testament lends strong support for identifying the seed of the woman as Christ. At the cross Christ triumphed over Satan, bruising his head (John 16:11; Col. 2:15). Even Galatians 3:16 refers to Christ as the singular Seed, in this case, the Descendant of Abraham.[3]

Satan's Temptation of Christ (Matt.4:1–11; Mark 1:12–13; Luke 4:1–13)

Jesus the Savior, and Satan, the sinner of all sinners—two entirely opposite persons—faced each other in the forty-day Temptation. This confrontation was under the leadership of the Spirit of God Himself, for Jesus was "led up by the Spirit into the wilderness to be tempted by the devil" (Matt. 4:1).

A moment's reflection brings to mind a number of contrasts between the Savior and Satan. Christ is the eternal uncreated One who is "before all things, and in Him all things hold together" (Col. 1:17) and who is also the Creator (John 1:3, 14; Col. 1:15; Heb 1:2). Satan is a creature (Ezek. 28:15) and therefore had a beginning in time. Christ is the all-knowing (John 1:48), all-powerful (Phil. 3:21), and everywhere-present One (John 14:23), but Satan possesses none of these perfections of God. The Savior was, of course, the sinless One (2 Cor. 5:21), and Satan was the one who committed the very first sin in the universe.

Christ and Satan are also opposites in their purposes. Christ came to redeem mankind, to give eternal life, and to enable His own to be victorious over sin in their lives. Satan, on the other hand, purposes to deceive people, to mimic God, and to chain people by sin and in sin. In other words, our Lord Jesus is the Savior of sinners, and Satan is the leader of the damned and the promoter of sin.

It is commonly said that the Savior was confronted with three different temptations from Satan in the wilderness experience. I believe it is better to view the three solicitations of Satan as three different attempts to get the Savior to commit the one sin of acting independently of God the Father's will for Him. After all, Satan himself had sinned by acting independently of God, as seen in his "I wills" (Isa. 14:13–14). He then got our first parents to act independently of God's will for them (Gen. 3). Throughout Old Testament history the story is repeated over and over: In sinning, people are rebelling against God and His will.

In seeking to get Jesus to act independently of the Father's will for Him, Satan took three approaches. First, he challenged the Son of God to turn the stones to bread to satisfy His hunger (Matt. 4:3). Christ had the power to do this, but to make those stones bread at that time would have been to disregard the Father's will that He fast there for forty days and forty nights.

Second, Satan challenged the Son of God's confidence in God the Father. He urged Christ to throw Himself down from the highest point of the temple and be protected from harm by angels (4:5–6). This was a call for Christ to take matters in His own hands rather than wait for the Father's timing.

Third, Satan challenged the Son of God to disregard the Father's will for the Savior's crucifixion and His exaltation as the object of worship. After Satan showed Jesus all the kingdoms of the world from a high mountain, he said, "All these things will I give you, if you fall down and worship me" (4:9). Here was an offer of a shortcut to divine destiny. Christ could avoid the Cross by worshiping Satan. Jesus did not challenge Satan's claim that he had the kingdoms of the world to give to Him, for Satan is, as Jesus said, "the prince of this world" (John 12:31 NIV; 14:30 NIV; 16:11 NIV). But for Christ to worship Satan would fulfill the devil's desire to exalt himself above God (Isa.14:13–14) and would totally pervert God's purposes. Imagine God worshiping Satan!

The Savior answered each of Satan's three challenges by quoting Scripture. The devil had distorted God's will as presented in Scripture. But Jesus' answers affirmed the truth of Scripture.

Just before His confrontation with Satan, Jesus identified Himself by baptism with His forerunner John the Baptist and his message. At that time the Father's voice from heaven was heard, "This is My beloved Son, in whom I am well-pleased" (Matt. 3:17). The Savior's victory over Satan's temptation demonstrated that He is indeed the beloved Son of God.

Jesus did not sin by succumbing to Satan's temptations, nor did He ever sin. But *could* He have sinned? The question of whether He was peccable, that is, *able not* to sin, or impeccable, that is, *not able* to sin, has been the subject of debate for a long time.[4] My own view of this issue can be summarized this way: If Christ's humanity is considered apart from His deity (just for the purpose of answering the question before us), it must be said that He was both temptable and peccable. On the other hand, if Christ's deity is considered apart from His humanity, we must say He was neither temptable nor peccable. Since deity and humanity are uniquely and perfectly united in Christ and can never be separated, He was tempted because He was man and He could not sin because He was God.

Because of the Savior's finished work on the cross, verified by His resurrection from the dead, Satan is a defeated foe. As Jesus said, "The ruler of this world has been judged" (John 16:11). His ultimate doom has been sealed. Announcing the completion of His work of redemption while on the cross, the Savior declared, "It is finished" (19:30). What He completed was His defeat of Satan and His provision of redemption for mankind. The Judge of all the universe demonstrated His victory over Satan by coming forth from the grave on the third day, just as He said He would. This sentence of judgment on Satan, procured and announced at the cross, will be executed when he is cast into the lake of fire prepared for him (Rev. 20:10). Meanwhile Satan roams about like a roaring lion seeking whom he may gobble up. He is presently "alive and well" on planet earth, but his days are numbered by God.

SATAN AND THE SAINTS OF GOD

The Saints' Opposition from Satan

As Christians seek to live according to Scripture they need to know that Satan and his evil angels are fighting against them. Believers also need to realize they cannot be successful in their own strength in opposing these supernatural opponents. These two realities are as basic and fundamental to the spiritual life as food and water are to one's physical life. Throughout their lives they are engaged in a series of battles against Satan, the enemy of God and His people. This spiritual struggle is not new to this age. It has always raged, from the Garden of Eden in Genesis to our day. Throughout the Bible we see evidence of Satan's recurring opposition to God's saints.

We do not know how much Satan knows. But we can be sure he is not omniscient; he does not know everything. He is not God's equal in this or in anything else. The fact that he is a creature means he has limitations. No doubt Satan knows he cannot remove Christians from the family of God, just as he knows he cannot triumph over God. Therefore his nefarious work against God's children is not to try to keep them out of heaven. What Satan *does* constantly work at is to keep believers from leading lives pleasing to God. In short, he wants to make a spiritual failure out of each of us. Just as he tried to get Christ to act independently of God, so he seeks to get us to live independently of God and His Word.

Each believer has three enemies—the devil, the flesh, and the world.[5] Usually this triumvirate of opposition against every child of God is presented in a different order: the world, the flesh, and the devil. I think the devil should be discussed first, not last, because he is enemy number one and he uses the flesh and the world in his insidious attempts to defeat God's people.

The devil. Satan is the master of deceit. Appearing as an angel of light, he is really an angel of darkness. Paul said Satan "hindered" him in his work (1 Thess. 2:18 KJV). And he expressed concern that Satan not take advantage of the Corinthian Christians (2 Cor. 2:11). The Greek world for "take advantage" means to defraud someone "often through trickery and treacherous means."[6] As the epitome of wickedness, the devil always seeks to frustrate God's work in believers' lives. Our downfall is his highest concern.

Peter, like Paul, knew firsthand of the devil's vicious ways. He described him as a roaring lion prowling around seeking someone to devour (1 Pet. 5:8). Paul told the Ephesian Christians the only way believers can be victorious over Satan is by putting on God's armor (Eph. 6:11–18). Paul did not say defeating Satan required deliverance from demons. Victory in spiritual warfare comes, he said, not by being delivered from demons, but by exercising our wills in opposing Satan with the armor God Himself provides. Later we will discuss this armor more.

Through the lust of the flesh Satan seeks to get us to misuse our God-given physical appetites. He tempts us to impurity of life, overindulgence in food and drink, improper expenditure of time and money, or any combination of these. Living in an age given to hedonism and materialism, believers must guard against sin in these areas. Christians need to remember that their bodies are the temples of the Holy Spirit (1 Cor. 6:19–20).

Many sinful things are in the world around us. Through the lust of the eyes people often entertain impure thoughts (Matt. 5:28). Our sex-mad world makes everyone susceptible to temptation and sin. The lust of the eyes involves more than sex, however. A craving for more and more material things is also common in our affluent society. It is still sin to covet and to place undue emphasis on things which of course will pass away. The philosophy of the world—"eat, drink, and be merry" (Luke 12:19), has become so glamorized that many Christians unwittingly have adopted it.

Perhaps believers are more susceptible to the pride of life than to either of the other two areas of Satan's attacks. Even Christians who are busy serving the Lord often fall prey to this trick of Satan. This is the "I love myself" attitude. It finds expression when one thinks no one else can do anything as well as he can. This is thinking more highly of oneself than he or she ought to think (Rom. 12:3). In short, it spells pride. Often this attitude becomes evident to others in words and actions.

The flesh. Paul used this term to refer to believers' capacity and tendency to sin (Rom. 7:18). It is sometimes spoken of as the sin nature. A child of God does not have two personalities within him, each battling for attention. However, each believer does have two natures—the old Adamic nature and the new nature received at the time of salvation.[7]

Many believe the apostle Paul's description in Romans 7 of his struggle to do what he knew he should do and not do the things he knew he should not do illustrates the experience of every believer. In his letter to the Galatians Paul pointed out that all Christians struggle with the flesh. "For the flesh sets its desire against the Spirit, and the Spirit against the flesh; for these are in opposition to one another, so that you may not do the things that you please" (Gal. 5:17).

The believer does have an enemy within. What we call it—the flesh, the old nature, a sinful disposition, or something else—is not the primary concern. The reason Christians struggle with sin in their lives is because of the presence of the old capacities and tendencies to sin.

The world. One of the Greek words translated "world" is *cosmos.* The word stresses order and organization. It is Satan's organized system or world-view that leaves God out and opposes Him. Because the world is at odds with God, Jesus told His disciples they would have continual conflict with it (John 15:18–20; 16:1–3). He also made it clear that the world hates believers who live for Christ (17:14).

Satan uses the attraction of the world to lure believers into his net. Since believers are not of this world, they are not to love it (1 John 2:15).

The world's hatred for believers manifests itself in various ways. It is not always in a direct and violent way. More often it is in subtle and insidious ways. Satan's anti-God philosophy is evident, for example, in every phase of modern education, much of which is built on an evolutionary hypothesis. Hatred makes itself known in the business world, social life, the entertainment world, and even in religion.

We should be careful not to adopt the philosophy that seeks to make Christianity compatible with the world. Biblical Christianity does not parallel the philosophy of the world. It intersects it at every turn. The world is in opposition to the Christian view of God and the world.

Victory over these formidable foes may seem impossible. Our enemy is characterized by wicked supernaturalism. Satan, though not God's equal, has tremendous power through the use of his wicked angels. He also uses the flesh and the world to take us captive. No believer is a match for him. Defeat is inevitable apart from the great and gracious provisions God has made for His people. These sources of victory are not for just a select few but for all in the family of God.

The Saints' Means of Victory over Satan

The work of God the Son. Many were the accomplishments of Christ in His death. The one on which all the others depend, of course, was His substitutionary atonement for sin and sinners. Our Lord did not die merely to show people how brave we should be when we die. Nor did He die as a victim of the unbelieving Jews and Romans. Instead, He died in the place of sinners, as their Substitute. Unless a person accepts this substitutionary work by faith, he will not be saved. The substitution is complete and final, however, even if none ever receive it. It is a reality and its value does not depend on its being received.

What is often overlooked is that the substitutionary work of Christ, which alone can bring salvation, is the same work that provides for the believer's cleansing from daily sin and victory over Satan and His demons in the Christian life. Believers have no other court of appeal, no other means of cleansing, no other source for victory, except the cross of Christ. The victory He achieved through His death over Satan and all the demons of hell two thousand years ago is the source of victory for every Christian since then.

Christ's presence with believers is just as real now as it was when He was here on earth. He promised, "I am with you always" (Matt. 28:20), and "I will never desert you, nor will I ever forsake you" (Heb. 13:5). However, we often fail to appropriate Christ's victory as our own. We fail to claim by faith all we have in Him.

Paul sensed that the Ephesian Christians were lacking in this area. So he told them to "put on the full armor of God, that you will be able to stand firm against the schemes of the devil" (Eph. 6:11). At the same time the apostle addressed the real opposition believers face. "Our struggle is . . . against the rulers, against the powers, against the world forces of this darkness, against the spiritual forces of wickedness in the heavenly places" (6:12).

The "full armor of God" (6:13), which believers are to put on, consists of six things: the belt of truth, the breastplate of righteousness, feet shod with the gospel of peace, the shield of faith, the helmet of salvation, and the sword of the Spirit (6:14–17). Prayer in the Spirit, Paul added, must accompany the armor (6:18).

What Paul really told the Ephesians to do as they battle against Satan and his angels was to put on Christ. As he told the Roman Christians, "But put on the Lord Jesus Christ, and make no provision for the flesh in regard to its lusts" (Rom. 13:14).[8]

The work of God the Holy Spirit. At the time of salvation the Holy Spirit takes up permanent residence in each believer (1 Cor. 6:19). We call this the indwelling of the Spirit. Jesus told His disciples, "I will ask the Father, and He will give you another Helper, that He may be with you forever; that is the Spirit of truth, whom the world cannot receive, because it does not behold Him or know Him, but you know Him because He abides with you, and will be in you" (John 14:16–17).

The Spirit's presence in and with the child of God is his or her source of strength and victory against all the satanic and demonic opposition against him. Jesus said the Spirit would teach those He indwells of the things of Christ (14:26) and guide God's people "into all the truth" (16:13). This includes the truth of all Christ did and is doing for us and also the truth about Satan's deceptive ways. The Spirit does all this by means of the Scriptures. This means we need to be constantly exposed to God's Word. The Bible states two negative commands and two positive commands that, when obeyed, enable us to benefit from the Spirit's presence in us.

First, God's children are told not to grieve the Spirit (Eph. 4:30). This means we are not to hurt or offend Him by sin. When we sin, the Spirit convicts us, thereby drawing our attention to the fact that it is wrong. When we ignore or suppress this work of the Spirit, we grieve Him.

Second, believers are not to "quench the Spirit" (1 Thess. 5:19). To quench means to suppress or stifle. We do this to the indwelling Holy Spirit when we say no to His ministry to our hearts. In other words, sin quenches the Spirit; it stifles His work in and through us.

Third, Scripture exhorts believers to "be filled with the Spirit" (Eph. 5:18). This means to be controlled by Him. We can never get more of the Holy Spirit than we received at the time of salvation, but we can give Him more of ourselves. The negative side of the command in this verse is, "Do not be drunk with wine." When a person is drunk, he is under wine's control. Similarly, believers are to be controlled by the Holy Spirit. When they are, Satan and his army of demons are unable to get a foothold on them.

Fourth, God's children are to "walk by the Spirit" (Gal. 5:16). In physical walking each new step we take depends on the previous step if we are to maintain our balance. So the metaphor Paul used here tells us we are to "walk" (i.e., conduct our lives) in complete dependence on the Spirit of God.

These two negative and two positive commands cannot be understood or obeyed apart from the Word of God. Only by obeying the Word can we avoid grieving or quenching the Spirit. And only by obeying the Word can we be controlled by the Spirit and live in dependence on Him.

In addition to the work of God the Son and God the Holy Spirit there is another great provision for victory over Satan and demons.

The work of the Word of God. Both the incarnate Word and the inspired Word are God's provision for every child of God to do battle with Satan. We have already seen how God the Son, the living Word, equips us for the conflict. Now it is important to note that the Scriptures, the written Word, do the same.

It is impossible to be victorious in Christian living apart from God's Word. Before discussing how God's truth arms us for conflict with the devil, the world, and the flesh, we note that it was through the Word that our new life in Christ began: "In the exercise of His will He brought us forth by the word of truth" (James 1:18). We were "born again . . . through the living and abiding word of God" (1 Pet. 1:23).

The "pure milk" of the Word enables us to "grow in respect to salvation" (1 Pet. 2:2). Conviction of sin comes about through the Word. God's Word convicts the believer of sin. It serves as a mirror, showing us our need (James 1:23–24). It is "able to judge the thoughts and intentions of the heart" (Heb. 4:12). Scripture provides cleansing for the child of God (John 15:3). Christ cleanses the church through the Word (Eph. 5:25–26). Guidance for the pilgrim-believer is found in God's Word (Ps. 40:8). The Word arms the believer against temptation (Matt. 4:1–11). It is the "sword of the Spirit" by which the believer is to do battle with Satan (Eph. 6:17). Through God's Word we are made sensitive to Satan and his vicious ways, because God's Word "is a lamp" to our feet (Ps. 119:105). The Word of God is used by the Spirit of God to equip God's people for service (2 Tim. 3:16–17).

However, the Bible is not a good-luck charm. It is not through the process of osmosis that these essentials for effective Christian living and service come to Christians. God's Word must be digested spiritually, just as the food we eat must be digested if it is to provide nourishment for our bodies. Therefore we need to read God's Word regularly (Acts 17:11), systematically (2 Tim. 2:15), prayerfully (Ps. 119:125), attentively (119:131), and obediently (John 15:10), and to know it thoroughly (2 Tim. 3:15; Jer. 15:16).

In this chapter we have learned of Satan's opposition to Christ the Savior and of his defeat at the Cross and the open tomb. We have learned too about Satan's hostility toward every child of God. He uses the lust of the world and the sin nature in each of us to seek our defeat. Satan is not

God's equal, but he does have hordes of demons to carry out his vile program. The threefold enemy each believer has is countered by the threefold work of God the Son, God the Holy Spirit, and the Word of God. We have been given an armor in Christ, but we must put it on. Whenever we do not wear it, Satan achieves the victory.

SATAN'S LIMITATIONS AND DESTINY

Today bookstores stock dozens of book titles on Satan and demons, especially in relation to believers. Much of the literature leaves the suggestion that Satan is God's equal. The two, God and Satan, are often viewed as engaged in some sort of global warfare, battling it out to determine who will be the victor. The outcome is left uncertain since it all depends on how successful Christians are in the spiritual warfare.

Such a view, however, is totally foreign to the Scriptures. The God of the Bible is sovereign, which means that Satan and his angels are all subject to Him. God is not seeking to be victorious over Satan. He already is. Though Satan is still active, he is a defeated foe. He has been condemned, but his "execution" is yet future.

This means Satan and his angels have definite limitations. They are fallen creatures. Everything they have ever done or will ever do has either been permitted by God or ordered by Him or both. They answer to God, not He to them. That is good for Christians to know.

Scripture exhorts us not to take Satan lightly. Even Michael the archangel "did not dare pronounce against [Satan] a railing judgment, but he said, 'The Lord rebuke you'" (Jude 9). If this counsel were heeded today, fewer people would be demanding that Satan and/or his demons do this or that.

Satan's limitations are also seen in the apostle John's word to believers: "Greater is He who is in you than he who is in the world" (1 John 4:4). The words "he who is in the world" clearly refer to Satan. The promised unceasing presence of Christ with each believer is assurance of victory over Satan (Heb. 13:5).

Each believer does have responsibilities with regard to God's provisions for doing battle with Satan. We are to be "alert" or watchful, because "the devil, prowls around like a roaring lion, seeking someone to devour" (1 Pet. 5:8). Never should a believer "give the devil an opportunity" (Eph. 4:27). In the immediate context of this command, anger, lying, stealing, and unwholesome talk among Christians are discussed, thereby suggesting that through these sins Satan is given opportunity to do his dirty work.

Satan can and should be resisted by God's people. In the strength and power of the Holy Spirit the child of God can "resist the devil" (James 4:7). When this command is obeyed, Satan "will flee from you." This resistance must be continuous because Satan's attacks are continuous. Before there can be true resistance to Satan, the believer must "submit ... to God (4:7)."

Satan's limitations are also evident from the fact that when we put on the armor God provides, we will be able to "stand firm against the schemes of the devil" (Eph. 6:11).

The eternal destiny of Satan and all his angels has also been addressed earlier. But this truth needs to be stated again. John, the apostle of love, put it bluntly: "And the devil who deceived them was thrown into the lake of fire and brimstone, where the beast and the false prophet are also; and they will be tormented day and night forever and ever" (Rev. 20:10). This eternal "home" for Satan is still future. He is not there yet. What John saw in his vision will come to pass after the future millennial reign of Christ on earth and after Satan will be allowed to "deceive the nations in the four corners of the earth" (20:8 NIV). When these nations gather around the city of Jerusalem, fire will come down from God out of heaven and devour them (20:9). Then the great deceiver will meet his eternal doom.

Jesus said this place of "eternal fire" was "prepared for the devil and his angels" (Matt. 25:41). We are not told when Satan's angels will be cast into this lake of fire, but it is reasonable to assume that it will be at the same time Satan will be cast there.

Jesus' Agony in the Garden
"Now an angel from heaven appeared to Him, strengthening Him." (Luke 22:43)

CHAPTER NINE
God's Son and God's Angels

⸻

T HIS CHAPTER examines the close relationships between Christ, God's Son, and God's holy angels. This is important to note because today people seldom distinguish between Christ and angels. Before we look at these relationships, we must be sure to understand that the Lord Jesus Christ is the eternal Son of God. At no point in time did He *become* God's Son. His Sonship is as eternal as His existence. In the New Testament that fact that Christ is God's Son always points to His deity, the fact that He is God.[1] This issue was discussed earlier in chapter 5.

THE MINISTRIES OF GOD'S ANGELS
TO AND FOR GOD'S SON

Scripture records more instances of angels ministering to Christ than to anyone else. The long list that follows reveals the reality of the ministry of holy angels to and for Christ the Son of God and also the extent of it.

The Angelic Announcement concerning the Birth of John the Baptist

Zacharias, a priest "of the division of Abijah," and his wife Elizabeth, "from the daughters of Aaron" (Luke 1:5), were godly people "advanced in years"

119

(1:7) and without children. One day while Zacharias was carrying out his duties as an Old Testament priest, "an angel of the Lord appeared to him" (1:11).

Zacharias was frightened by the strange appearance but was calmed by the angel and told not to be afraid. The angel then said to him, "Your petition has been heard, and your wife Elizabeth will bear you a son, and you will give him the name John" (1:13). The angel also told Zacharias the son to be born to his barren and aged wife would be "filled with the Holy Spirit" (1:15) even before his birth. Most importantly, the son to be named John would "go as a forerunner" before Jesus "in the spirit and power of Elijah, to turn the hearts of the fathers back to the children, and the disobedient to the attitude of the righteous; so as to make ready a people prepared for the Lord" (1:17).

Naturally, Zacharias asked the angel Gabriel how he would realize this, given his and Elizabeth's ages. The angel responded by telling Zacharias he would be unable to speak until "these things take place" (1:20). And that is exactly what happened because of his unbelief.

We see from this visit of Gabriel that angelic ministry about Christ began even before He was born of Mary.

The Angelic Announcement concerning the Birth of Jesus

Later God sent the same angel Gabriel on another mission. This time the visit was to the Virgin Mary. The angel found her in Nazareth, greeted her, and said to her, "Hail, favored one! The Lord is with you" (Luke 1:28). Mary was disturbed by this salutation, but Gabriel calmed her fears and told her she would conceive and bear a son, whose name would be Jesus (1:31). He would be "the Son of the Most High" to whom would be given "the throne of His father David" (1:32).

Mary then became even more alarmed. Since "I am a virgin" (1:34), she asked, "How can this be?" The angel told Mary she would conceive as no other woman ever had or would. The Holy Spirit would overshadow her and cause the conception miraculously without any male involvement (1:35). Gabriel then told Mary about his visit to Elizabeth and her conception. After Mary acknowledged herself as a "bondslave of the Lord" (1:38), Gabriel left.

Just as the angel Gabriel had said, John the Baptist and Jesus were born, both in miraculous ways. God the Father had employed His angel Gabriel to announce the coming births both of His Son's forerunner and of His Son.

The Angelic Instruction to Joseph

Joseph, to whom Mary was engaged, was distressed by her pregnancy because he had not had sexual relations with her. About the time he considered sending her away secretly, thinking she had been unfaithful to him, "an angel of the Lord appeared to him in a dream" (Matt. 1:20). Presumably this angel also was Gabriel. Joseph was told not to be afraid and to take Mary to be his wife, because the child who "has been conceived in her is of the Holy Spirit" (1:20).

Joseph awoke from his sleep and "did as the angel of the Lord commanded him, and took her as his wife, but kept her a virgin until she gave birth to a Son; and he called His name Jesus" (1:24–25).

Angels were used to prepare the way for the birth of the Christ child.

The Angelic Announcement to the Shepherds

The time had come. The Son of God was about to be born into the world. Caesar Augustus probably did not know and certainly did not care about the promise to Mary and Joseph about the coming birth of Jesus. The monarch ordered a census to be taken, which meant that Joseph and his wife, who was soon to give birth, had to go from Nazareth to Bethlehem to register. And "while they were there, the days were completed for her to give birth. And she gave birth to her firstborn son" (Luke 2:6–7).

At this time some shepherds were out all night on the Judean hills keeping watch over their flocks of sheep. If there was any sleep in them, it left suddenly. "An angel of the Lord suddenly stood before them, and the glory of the Lord shone around them; and they were terribly frightened" (2:9).

Just as an angel had told Zacharias, Mary, and Joseph not to be afraid, this angel told shepherds the same thing. He said this event was good news because the "Savior who is Christ the Lord" (2:11) had been born in the city of David (i.e., Bethlehem, the same city where David had been born centuries earlier; 1 Sam. 16:1; 17:12).

The angel who first appeared was then joined by "a multitude of the heavenly host praising God" (Luke 2:13). After the angels left, the shepherds made their way to Bethlehem to see for themselves.

The Second Angelic Announcement to Joseph

Magi or wise men came from the east to Jerusalem seeking the One who was born "King of the Jews" (Matt. 2:2). These men were professionals who studied stars. They came to Jerusalem because they "saw His star in the east" (2:2).

King Herod was troubled by this and consulted with the Jewish leaders as to where the Messiah was to be born. When Herod was told His birthplace, he secretly called the Magi and found out exactly when the star had appeared. Herod then told them to go to Bethlehem and find the Child and come back and tell him so he, too, could go and worship Him (2:8). The Magi found Jesus and gave Him their gifts. Then God warned them in a dream not to go back to Herod.

After the wise men left, an angel again visited Joseph in a dream, and told him, "Take the Child and His mother, and flee to Egypt, and remain there until I tell you" (2:13). Joseph followed the instructions of the angel. Once again, God called on one of His angels to minister for Him.

The Angelic Ministry to Christ at the Time of His Temptation

Our Lord was led by the Holy Spirit to a place in the desert where He was tempted by the devil (Matt. 4:1–10). In three ways, as we have seen, Satan tried to get Christ to act independently of the Father's will for Him. Jesus responded each time by refusing Satan's solicitations to sin and quoting Old Testament Scripture to defend His actions.

Satan left Christ just as he found Him—the sinless, spotless Savior. When the devil left Him, "angels came and began to minister to Him" (4:11). Who sent them? Most certainly, God the Father did.

The Angelic Ministry to Christ in Gethsemane

When Christ led eleven of His disciples "to a place called Gethsemane," He took Peter, James, and John with Him to a remote place in the garden. He told them to "keep watch" (Matt. 26:36–38) with Him, but they fell asleep. Three times He interrupted His praying to check on them, and they were sleeping. As He was alone praying fervently, "His sweat became like drops of blood, falling down upon the ground" (Luke 22:44). At that time "an angel from heaven appeared to Him, strengthening Him" (22:43).

Judas Iscariot and a large crowd with him came to where Jesus and the disciples were. Judas identified Jesus to the religious leaders by kissing Him, and they arrested Him (22:47–50).

Peter was wide awake by this time. He pulled out his sword and struck the high priest's servant, cutting off his ear. It is usually thought Peter really intended to kill the slave with a head wound but missed his target. Jesus' response to Peter gives another insight into what was most certainly the case throughout His entire life on earth. He said, "Do you think that I cannot appeal to My Father, and He will at once put at My disposal more than twelve legions of angels?" (Matt. 26:53).

Roman legions included between three thousand and six thousand soldiers. Thus twelve legions would total between 36,000 and 72,000. However, Jesus was not intending to give an exact number of angels whom He could beckon. His point was that a very large number, a number more than sufficient for the task, would be sent by His Father if He asked for them.

The Angelic Ministry at Christ's Empty Tomb

On the third day after Christ's death an angel of the Lord rolled away the huge stone the soldiers had placed at the tomb's entrance. The angel's appearance was blindingly brilliant, white as snow. The guards whom the authorities stationed there saw the angel, were visibly shaken, and "became like dead men" (Matt. 28:4). They "froze in their tracks," we would say today.

The angel then spoke to the two Marys who had come to complete the anointing of their Lord's body. The angel told them not to be afraid and added, "He is not here, for He has risen, just as He said" (28:6).

After Peter and John arrived at the tomb, they left to tell the other disciples the tomb was empty (John 20:1–9). After they left, Mary stayed outside the tomb and wept. As she stooped and looked inside, she saw two angels dressed in white, one seated at each end of the place where Jesus' body had been lying (20:12). When the angels asked Mary why she was sad, she told them it was because she could not find the Lord.

The Angelic Ministry at Christ's Ascension

For forty days after Christ's resurrection He gave "many convincing proofs" (Acts 1:3) to His own of His completed and victorious life and death. Then the Lord led them to Bethany, lifted His hands, blessed them, and ascended back to the Father (Luke 24:50–51). "He was lifted up while they were looking on, and a cloud received Him out of their sight" (Acts 1:9). "While He ascended by His own divine power, we read that He was 'carried up into heaven,' a fact indicating that angels attended Him and formed His chariot, just as they did for Elijah when he was carried up in a chariot of fire to heaven (Ps. 68:17–18; Acts 1:10–11)."[2]

As Jesus ascended to heaven, two angels, "men in white clothing," spoke to the stunned disciples and said, "This Jesus, who has been taken up from you into heaven, will come in just the same way as you have watched Him go into heaven" (1:10–11).

The Angelic Ministry in Heaven Magnifying Christ

When John was on Patmos Island, he saw a vision of God on His throne in heaven. God held a book or scroll sealed with seven seals (Rev. 5:1). John also saw and heard "a strong angel proclaiming with a loud voice, 'Who is worthy to open the book and to break its seals?'" (5:2). No one in heaven, on the earth, or even under the earth was qualified to break the seals and open the book.

In his vision John began to weep because no one could be found to reveal what was in the book. Finally, John saw Christ the Lamb of God, who came and took the book from the Father's hand (5:3–7). All of heaven's occupants began to praise the Son of God, who alone was worthy to open the book and release the awful judgments revealed in it.

Included in the heavenly chorus was the voice of many angels around the throne: "the number of them was myriads of myriads, and thousands of thousands" (5:11). What were these holy angels doing? They were doing what they have always done and are still doing—magnifying God's Son.

The Angelic Ministry to John about Christ

At both the beginning and the end of the Book of Revelation we are told that the revelation John received on Patmos was "the Revelation of Jesus Christ" and was given to him by Christ's angel (Rev. 1:1; 22:16).[3]

It is a truth often overlooked that God employed His angels to be channels of His revelation to man. In fact, major bodies of Scripture are said to have been administered to humans by angels, including the Mosaic Law (Gal. 3:19; Heb. 2:2; Acts 7:53); the Book of Revelation (Rev. 1:1; 22:16); and the visions given to Daniel (Dan. 7:15–27; 8:13–26; 9:20–27).

The Angelic Ministry at the Return of Christ

Angels will be involved both at the Rapture, when Christ will meet believers of this age in the air to take them to heaven, and also when He comes with His own to the earth to establish His kingdom.

Before the awful Day of the Lord begins on earth, Christ will descend from heaven while five heavenly and earthly "commotions" will take place. From heaven there will be the shout, the voice of the archangel, and the trumpet of God (1 Thess. 4:16). On the earth the "dead in Christ" will rise and then believers who will be alive on the earth will "be caught up together with them in the clouds to meet the Lord in the air."

The archangel, probably Michael, will represent all the holy angels who will accompany Christ's return for His own.

At Christ's second coming to the earth, at least seven years after His return at the Rapture, God's angels will also be involved. In fact, Christ Himself said that when He comes in His glory, all the angels will be with Him (Matt. 25:31; Mark 8:38). Precisely what they will do, we are not told. Based on what God's angels have always done with respect to God's Son, we may assume they will be serving Him while they magnify Him.

One final ministry of God's angels for God's Son involves their executing judgment on unbelievers when He returns to the earth to establish His millennial reign. As Matthew wrote, at the end of the age "the angels shall come forth, and take out the wicked from among the righteous, and will cast them into the furnace of fire; there shall be weeping and gnashing of teeth" (Matt. 13:49–50).

GOD'S SON AND GOD'S ANGELS IN HEBREWS 1–2

No study of what the Bible teaches about angels would be complete without reference to Hebrews 1–2. These chapters constitute the most extensive single body of Scripture dealing with angels. The primary focus of these chapters lies on the vast superiority of Christ over angels. Their ministry and service to Him and for Him are also included in the chapters.

It will be helpful to see the major point of the Book of Hebrews first. When that is noted, then the contribution of Hebrews 1–2 to the whole book becomes clearer.

The Book of Hebrews was written to people with a Jewish background. Several things in the book—beginning with the title in the Greek manuscript "To the Hebrews"—point to this conclusion. More than that, it was written to Jews who had come to faith in Christ but needed to "go on" in their walk with God. They were tempted to revert to the Levitical system of sacrifices.

The purpose of the human writer was to convince his readers that in His person and work Christ is superior to anyone and everything in the old Mosaic system. Since they had begun to drift back, the writer urged them to advance spiritually (Heb. 6:1). They were to do so by noting the superiority of Christ to the Old Testament prophets (1:1–3), the angels (1:4–14; 2:5–18), Moses (3:1–6), Joshua (4:2–10), Aaron (4:14–5:10), the Levitical priesthood (7:1–28), the Old Covenant (8:1–13), and the old ordinances and sacrifices (9:1–10:18).

Hebrews spells out seven reasons why Christ is superior to angels. (1) He has a more excellent name than angels do (1:4–5). He is the Son of

God; angels are only God's servants, not His equals. (2) God's angels worship God's Son (1:6), and they are never to be worshiped. (3) God's angels are creatures created by God's Son who is the uncreated One (1:7). (4) The Father called God's Son "God," and even in His incarnate state He had greater gifts than angels (1:8–9). (5) The angels are servants of God, but Christ is God's Son and the divine Servant of Yahweh (1:14). (6) The Word of God did not originate with angels. They were simply used of God to give His message to man, whereas the word was spoken by "the Lord" (2:2–3). (7) In the future Millennium, Christ, not angels, will rule (2:5–7).

Garrett gives a fitting summary of the contribution of Hebrews 1–2 to the superiority of God's Son to His angels.

> For our purposes, this text shows that the Bible regards angels as secondary, even incidental, figures in comparison to the Son of God. They have neither His power nor His position. They are servants where He is God. More than that, He excels them in love and humility, in that He allowed Himself for a time to become lower than the angels for humanity's sake (Heb. 2:9). Unlike angels, the Son of God knows what it is to be human.
>
> The folly of the current craze over angels could not be more pronounced. People prefer lesser spirits to the creator of all spirits. They seek revelation from angels rather than learning from the final revelation in the Son. If we reject God, to which one of the angels shall we turn for help?[4]

Jesus Healing the Man Possessed with a Demon
"And amazement came upon them all, and they began discussing with one another saying,
'What is this message? For with authority and power He commands the unclean spirits,
and they come out.'" (Luke 4:36)

CHAPTER TEN
Demon Possession in the New Testament

THE CHRISTIAN COMMUNITY is divided over the subjects of this
chapter and the next one. The disagreement is not so much over the
fact that in New Testament times demons did possess people and were
cast out, but rather over who, if anyone, can be demon-possessed today.
If demons do possess people today, can they or can they not be exorcised?

Demon possession was rather widespread during Christ's life on earth.
Demons actually took up residence in people, we are told. Jesus cast them
out of a number of individuals. In the Gospels those who were possessed
of demons had various physical and/or emotional maladies, such as dumbness, blindness, convulsions, self-destructiveness, superhuman strength,
and even insanity. As noted earlier, Scripture distinguishes between those
physical illnesses caused by demon possession and those not caused by it
(Matt. 4:24; Luke 7:21).

Why emphasize the New Testament in our discussion on demon possession? The reason is that the Old Testament has no clear undisputed
references to demons possessing people, while the Gospels include a large
number of references to demons being cast out of people. In Acts and the
Epistles there is very little discussion about this demonic activity. A legiti-
mate question is, Why is this the case? We will try to throw some light on
the answer to that question as we proceed.

But first, what is demon possession and how is it to be distinguished from other things demons did in New Testament times?

THE MEANING OF DEMON POSSESSION

Descriptive New Testament Words

The expression most often used for demon possession[1] is the Greek word *echō*, "to have." For example, "He has an unclean spirit" (Mark 3:30); "He has a demon" (Luke 7:33); "You have a demon" (John 7:20); and "many who had unclean spirits" (Acts 8:7). This was the way people of that time referred to one who was possessed of a demon or demons. Such expressions are used only in the Gospels and in Acts.

The verb *daimonizomai*, "to be demon-possessed," is used thirteen times, all of them in the Gospels—seven times in Matthew, four times in Mark, once in Luke, and once in John. This word is used only rarely outside the New Testament. It is never used in the New Testament to describe demonic influence which the victim could resist. Rather, the word describes the control a demon had over an individual, oppression that he or she could not successfully withstand alone.

Thus, "demon possession" is a better translation of *daimonizomai* than "demonized."[2] It is used only in the sense of actual demonic possession, not of demonic influence.

The phrase "with an unclean spirit" describes two individuals who were demon-possessed (Mark 1:23; 5:2). To be "demon-possessed" and to be "with an unclean spirit" mean the same thing; both descriptions are used of the man from the Gerasenes (Mark 5:2, 15, 18). Luke described him both ways as well (Luke 8:27, 36).

Alex Konya has well summarized the New Testament teaching on the meaning of demon possession: It is "the invasion of a victim's body by a demon (or demons), in which the demon exercises living and sovereign control over the victim, which the victim cannot successfully resist."[3]

One is demon-possessed when a demon (or demons) takes up residence in that person's body, resulting in degrees of derangement and the inability of the possessed to free himself or herself from demonic control.

Distinction between Demon Possession and Demon Influence

Demon possession and demon influence are related but are not the same. Demon possession is more than demon influence. Influence describes the general work of demons against God and His people. It is both constant and continuous. Possession occurs when the demons go beyond exerting influence and actually indwell their victims. Whether their evil work involves influence or possession, they can operate only by God's permission. They are not sovereign, nor are they God's equals.

Merrill F. Unger draws distinctions between demon influence and demon possession in this way: "In demon influence, evil spirits exert power over a person short of actual possession. Such influence may vary from mild harassment to extreme subjection when body and mind become dominated and held in slavery by spirit agents. Christians, as well as non-Christians, can be so influenced. They may be oppressed, vexed, depressed, hindered, and bound by demons."[4]

The People Possessed by Demons

The New Testament records instances of a number of people who were said to be demon-possessed. The spiritual state of these people is not specified. In none of the examples are the victims clearly distinguished as believers. It follows, therefore, that we cannot determine from the examples whether those possessed were believers or not.

Evangelicals differ on this issue. Some argue that both believers and unbelievers were demon-possessed in New Testament times, and both can still be possessed by demons today. Others insist that only unbelievers were possessed in New Testament times and can be today. The arguments on both sides must come from other considerations than the New Testament itself, since it does not tell us whether the demon-possessed were believers or nonbelievers.

Those who hold the view that believers were and still can be possessed usually refer to these Scripture passages to support their view: 1 Samuel 16:14; Luke 13:11–16; Acts 5:3; 1 Corinthians 5:5; 2 Corinthians 11:14; 12:7. Yet not one of them states specifically that demons took up residence in believers.

1 Samuel 16:14. "Now the Spirit of the LORD departed from Saul, and an evil spirit from the LORD terrorized him." The "evil spirit" that terrorized Saul is not said to indwell him. The torment he experienced could have been external. Furthermore, whether Saul was a believer is open to serious question.

Luke 13:11–16. "And behold, there was a woman who for eighteen years had had a sickness caused by a spirit; and she was bent double, and could not straighten up at all. And when Jesus saw her, He called her over and said to her, 'Woman, you are freed from your sickness.' And He laid His hands upon her; and immediately she was made erect again, and began glorifying God. . . . And this woman, a daughter of Abraham as she is, whom Satan has bound for eighteen long years, should she not have been released from this bond on the Sabbath day?' "

Some say the fact that Jesus called this woman "a daughter of Abraham" means she was a believer. But this is not necessarily the case. This term may simply describe her as a Jewess. Also the passage does not say a demon was in her, though it does say she was bound by Satan for eighteen years.

Acts 5:3. "But Peter said, 'Ananias, why has Satan filled your heart to lie to the Holy Spirit, and to keep back some of the price of the land?' " The word translated "filled" here is the same word used in Ephesians 5:18 in God's command for believers to be filled with the Spirit. The meaning in this latter passage is that the Spirit is to be allowed to control the believer in the same way strong drink controls those who consume it. The filling of the Spirit is not the same as the indwelling of the Spirit. That Ananias allowed Satan to control him in his deception about giving is not in question. But it is highly questionable that such control meant he was demon-possessed.

1 Corinthians 5:5. "I have decided to deliver such a one to Satan for the destruction of his flesh, that his spirit may be saved in the day of the Lord Jesus." Though Paul delivered to Satan a believer who was guilty of incest, nothing is said about demons. Surely the apostle was not saying that Satan would personally and permanently indwell this man.[5]

2 Corinthians 11:14; 12:7. "And no wonder, for even Satan disguises himself as an angel of light. . . . And because of the surpassing greatness of the revelations, for this reason, to keep me from exalting myself, there was given me a thorn in the flesh, a messenger of Satan to buffet me—to keep me from exalting myself!" These two verses present the weakest argument of all that demons possess believers, but they are used by those who hold this view. Charles Ryrie shows the fallacy of using these two verses to support the view that believers can be demon-possessed. "The 'different spirit' of 2 Corinthians 11:4 is not a demon any more than 'another Jesus' in the verse is. It is another gospel which brings bondage. The base of operation of the messenger of Satan (a demon) which God sent to afflict Paul is unstated in 12:7. Though the result was a thorn in the flesh, this did not mean that the demon had to reside in Paul."[6]

While demons certainly do influence God's children (which influence may at times provide responses similar to demon possession), I do not believe demons can indwell believers. Several reasons support this conclusion. First, none of the passages used to prove believers can be demon-possessed even use the words *demon* or *demons*. Second, none of those who were actually demon-possessed can be proven to be believers. Third, it is inconceivable that God the Father, God the Son, or the Holy Spirit would share their abode in believers with the demons of hell (2 Cor. 6:15–16).

THE NATURE OF DEMON POSSESSION

In chapter 7 we established from Scripture that demons are fallen angels, and they, like unfallen angels, have personality. Demons are spirit beings who are morally perverted. They are described as "unclean spirits" (Matt. 10:1; Luke 11:24), that is, they are morally and spiritually unclean. They are also called "spiritual forces of wickedness" (Eph. 6:12). Demons join Satan their leader in sowing tares among God's people (Matt. 13:37–42), assisting him in all his deceit and disguise.

These general descriptions of demons help us understand the nature of their possession of individuals. Several physical and emotional problems stemmed from demon possession. But they did not always result from demon possession. They can also be brought about by other things.

Physical and mental illnesses are the most common traits of demons indwelling people in the New Testament. The two men who met Jesus as He arrived in their country were "exceedingly violent" (Matt. 8:28). Everyone feared these two were demon-possessed. The boy who was brought to Jesus by his father was "mute" (Mark 9:17) because he was "possessed with a spirit." Blindness and dumbness were true of the man brought to Jesus to be healed of demons (Matt. 12:22). A demon-possessed girl suffered terribly (15:22). Another who had an unclean spirit screamed at Jesus (Mark 1:23, 26). Demon possession resulted in seizures slamming a boy to the ground and causing him to foam at the mouth, to grind his teeth, and to be stiff like a board (9:18–20). The man from the Gerasenes did the same and mutilated himself with stones as well (Mark 5:5). Demons who took up residence in people caused their victims to be "troubled" (Luke 6:18; Acts 5:16). One whom Jesus met who was possessed with demons had not worn clothing for a long time (Luke 8:27).

Torment is probably the best and most descriptive word to describe what demons did to those whom they indwelt. Another form of torment not included in the above is the personality change that demons brought about in their victims. In many of the New Testament cases it is difficult to distinguish between the voice of the demon and that of the victim. When demons spoke through individuals, they spoke in language easy to understand. In other words, what they said was logical and not just gibberish.

THE CAUSE OF DEMON POSSESSION

One of the notable facts about demon possession in the New Testament is that none who were inflicted in this way were rebuked or even scolded for it. Though Jesus did associate sickness with sin on at least two occasions (Matt. 9:2; John 5:14), He never associated demon possession with sin. This reality runs counter to much of what is being proclaimed today by many involved in so-called deliverance ministries. A number of writers say demon possession is caused by persistence in certain sins; a continued carnal state; using nonprescribed drugs or alcohol, horoscopes, or ouija boards; playing the "Dungeons and Dragons" game; listening to hard rock music; sexual sins; New Age channeling; involvement in Eastern religions; or ancestral influence.

The Bible does not tell us why people are sometimes possessed by demons. But it does give us two rather strong hints.

Two sins—idolatry and occultism[7]—seem to be possible avenues to demon possession. Three lines of evidence suggest that idolatry may lead to demon possession.[8] The first is from two Old Testament passages that refer to sacrificing to demons (Deut. 32:17; Ps. 106:36–37). In both cases idolatry and demonism were involved.

Second, Paul associated idolatry and demonism when he warned believers not to partake of pagan idol sacrifices. "No, but I say that the things which the Gentiles sacrifice, they sacrifice to demons, and not to God; and I do not want you to become sharers in demons. You cannot drink the cup of the Lord and the cup of demons; you cannot partake of the table of the Lord and the table of demons" (1 Cor. 10:20–21).

Third, most of the New Testament examples of demon possession were in areas that, like Galilee, were highly influenced by paganism. The only reference to demon possession close to Jerusalem is Peter's casting out of demons in Acts 5:16. John, who in his Gospel emphasized Jesus' ministry in and around Jerusalem, recorded no instances of demon possession.

The second sin linked with demon possession, perhaps as a cause, is occultic relationships.[9] Two passages in Acts suggest such a connection. In the first, Acts 16:16, a girl had "a spirit of divination." More literally the verse says she had "a spirit, a Python." This name came from the occultic oracle at Delphi or Pytho, the name of the town beneath Mount Parnassus in Greece. This girl was called a Python, and was a soothsayer. Some connection seems evident between the girl's involvement with magic and sorcery and her having a spirit of divination, the demonically induced ability to tell the future. The Greek work for "fortune-telling" in 16:16 is *manteuomenē*, a word with pagan connections, used only here in the New Testament. It suggests telling the future by means of consulting a demonic oracle.

The second passage that links demonism with the occult is Acts 19:8–20. Ephesus was known for its involvement in occultic practices in New Testament times. And it was here that Paul under the Spirit's guidance performed miracles and exorcisms (19:11–12, 13–16). One cannot help but wonder why exorcisms, the casting out of demons, seemed to be prevalent in the very area where occultism was popular.

When the gospel of God's saving grace reached Ephesus and many turned to Christ, they burned their magic literature, thereby showing they were truly repentant. Luke estimated these books to have been worth large sums of money (19:19). Theirs was a costly repentance.

These instances demonstrate a link between demon possession and idolatry and/or occultism. However, we should not conclude that demon possession *always* results from involvement with idolatry or the occult.

Do demons still inhabit human bodies today? The New Testament does not say demons would continue to take up residence in people. But then neither does it say specifically that holy angels would continue to minister to God's people in the present age.

Clearly, God's Word does teach the existence of good and bad angels. It also declares how in Bible times holy angels served God and evil angels served Satan. Since there is no scriptural teaching to the contrary we may assume that angels and demons continue to serve their respective masters. This would include bad angels, or demons, indwelling people. Since demons never possessed believers, we may be assured they do not do so now. Yet today demon possession of the unsaved may well occur occasionally.

Jesus Casts Out Demons

"And the demons entreated Him, saying, 'Send us into the swine so that we may enter them.' And He gave them permission. And coming out, the unclean spirits entered the swine; and the herd rushed down the steep bank into the sea, about two thousand of them; and they were drowned in the sea." (Mark 5:12–13)

CHAPTER ELEVEN
Demon Exorcism in the New Testament

∞∞∞

THE MEANING OF EXORCISM

SINCE WILLIAM BLATTY'S BOOK, *The Exorcist*, and the film with the same name, the terms *exorcist* and *exorcism* have become common-place. Neither of these terms, however, is ever used in the New Testament to describe Jesus' casting out of demons. That may be because His work of deliverance for those possessed by demons differed from that performed by Jews and others in His day. He did not use incantations, religious rites, or magical formulas as others did. He delivered the demon-possessed by a simple and direct command to the demons to come out—and the demons obeyed.

John Davis gives a helpful summary of the New Testament usage of the word *exorcist*. "The English word 'exorcist' is derived from the Greek verb *exorkizō* which is used only in Matthew 26:63 and the Septuagint version of Genesis 24:3. The word has the sense of charging with an oath or adjuring. The noun form (*exorkistōn*) is used in Acts 19:13 of certain Jewish 'exorcists' who attempted to imitate Paul's practice of casting out demons, but without success (cf. Acts 19:14–16). That there were a number of Jewish exorcists in Palestine at that time is clear from Matthew 12:27; Mark 9:38 and Luke 9:49–50."[1]

Peter Toon says nonbelievers sought to expel evil spirits by means of prayer, divination, or magic.[2] Jesus, however, exorcised demons by appealing to God's power. Bible-believers today who believe demon exorcism is still possible do the same.

Demon exorcism then means to cast demons out of those they inhabit, individuals in whose body the demons have taken up residence. The New Testament records a number of examples of exorcism.

EXORCISMS PERFORMED BY JESUS

Four exorcisms by Jesus are given extensive treatment in the New Testament.[3]

The Demon-Possessed Man in the Synagogue
(Mark 1:23–28; Luke 4:33–37)

The first miracle Mark and Luke record is Jesus' deliverance of the demoniac in the Capernaum synagogue. They both also associated the exorcism with Jesus' teaching in the synagogue. Mark and Luke also both state that later in the evening many who were sick and demon-possessed were brought to Jesus and He healed them and cast out their demons. Mark added that Jesus went throughout Galilee in the synagogues casting out demons (Mark 1:39).

We do not know why the man with the unclean spirit was in the synagogue. We do know, though, what the demon said through him when Jesus appeared. The demon screamed three things at Jesus—two questions and one affirmation.

The first question was, "What do we have to do with you, Jesus of Nazareth?" (Mark 1:24; cf. Luke 4:34). This and the second question must have been raised because of Jesus' authoritative message in the synagogue. The demon, representing his fellow-demons by using the plural "we," asked a question with an implied answer. By it, he was admitting he and his kind had nothing in common with Jesus.

Second, the demon said through his victim, "Have you come to destroy us?" (Mark 1:24; Luke 4:34). The implication behind this question is that the demons expected their kingdom to be destroyed by Jesus. Doubtless, the demon's reference was to Jesus' coming to earth, not just to the synagogue in Capernaum. The demon's question may also imply that the demons knew their ultimate defeat and final punishment were certain. What the demons wanted to know was whether that punishment was imminent.

Third, the demon acknowledged that he knew who Jesus is. "I know who you are," he said, "the Holy One of God" (Mark 1:24; Luke 4:34). The demon knew the source of Jesus' authority and miracle-working power. That was more than the Pharisees acknowledged. They instead said Christ performed His miracles in the power of "Beelzebul the ruler of the demons" (Matt. 12:24), under whom the demon speaking to Jesus worked.

After the demon's confession, Jesus gave him a command. The word "rebuked" (Mark 1:25) speaks of great authority behind the command. It calls attention to the subjugation of demons and therefore His control over them. The rebuke Jesus gave to the demon included a command to shut up and get out of the man. Our Lord certainly did not need or want the testimony of demons to His authority and messiahship.

There is a striking contrast between the way Jesus cast out demons, illustrated by this case, from the way many who claim to have "deliverance ministries" today carry on their work. Jesus did not bother to name the unclean spirit or "bind" him. Neither did He use any of the paraphernalia often associated with casting out demons today. He spoke, and it was done, just as He did when He created the world and Adam. (Gen. 1).

The Demon-Possessed Man from the Country of the Gerasenes
(Matt. 8:28–34; Mark 5:1–20; Luke 8:26–39)

All three accounts put this case of exorcism right after Jesus' storm-stilling miracle. Mark gave the most detailed account, and Matthew's account is even more abbreviated than Luke's.

After the miracle on the sea, when the disciples witnessed Jesus' mighty power over the forces of nature, Jesus was met by "a man from the tombs with an unclean spirit" (Mark 5:2). This incident includes three aspects. (1) The demon did not immediately obey Jesus' command to leave the man. (2) Jesus asked the demon's name. (3) Jesus even granted the demons' request to send them into the pigs nearby.[4]

Matthew mentioned that two who were demon-possessed came to Jesus, whereas Mark and Luke referred to one. If Mark or Luke had said there was *only* one demoniac, we would have a contradiction with Matthew's statement that there were two. However, Mark and Luke likely referred to one because this one was better known than the other or perhaps because he was more severely afflicted by the demons.

The demon-possessed man lived among the tombs. It is usually thought that he was not a Jew, because Jews would have thought of the place he lived to be unclean and also because of the herd of swine in the region. The fact that the demoniac called Jesus "Son of the Most High God" (5:7; Luke 8:28) and was told to herald the news of his deliverance to his family also fits a Gentile rather than a Jew.

This poor man, tormented by the demons, exhibited violent behavior and unusual strength (Mark 5:3–4). When he saw Jesus, he ran to seek His help. Much like the demon in the synagogue, this demon cried out to Jesus, "What do I have to do with You, Jesus, Son of the Most High God?" (5:7). This demon also begged Jesus not to torment him (5:7). This man, too, was possessed by more than one demon (5:9).

The demons in this man did not want to be sent out of the country (5:10); they preferred inhabiting the swine nearby (5:11–12). Jesus granted their request. The swine drowned in the sea, and the demons presumably went to indwell others.

The Demon-Possessed Daughter of the Syrophoenician Woman (Matt. 15:21–28; Mark 7:24–30)

It is highly significant that this grieving mother was a Gentile. Unlike many Jews, she, a Gentile, acknowledged that Jesus is the Son of David, that is, that He is the Messiah. No doubt this mother came to Jesus because she had heard of His miracle-working power which authenticated His claims to be Israel's Messiah and the world's Savior. Her daughter, even though young, was "cruelly demon possessed" (Matt. 15:22), and the mother believed Jesus could help her.

In the contexts of both Matthew's and Mark's accounts Jesus was in conflict with the Pharisees. What a contrast existed between these Jewish leaders, who refused to believe He is the Messiah, and this Gentile woman in need, who came to Him as the Messiah.

Jesus' first response to the woman's urgent request was to remind her that He had come as Israel's Messiah. He said that children who represented "the lost sheep of the house of Israel" (Matt. 10:6) must be fed or ministered to first (15:26). The woman readily acknowledged this and picked up on the word picture Jesus had drawn when He said, "It is not good to take the children's bread and throw it to the dogs" (15:26). The woman saw herself not as a child in the family of Israel but as a household dog. Interestingly this is how Jews often referred to Gentiles. In other words, she was not interested in getting what belonged to Israel but merely in receiving some of God's blessing.

Jesus responded because of her great faith and delivered her daughter on the spot without even seeing her. He pronounced her daughter whole, and when the mother got home, she found her delivered of the demon.

The Demon-Possessed Epileptic Boy
(Matt. 17:14–21; Mark 9:14–29; Luke 9:37–43)

The accounts of this miracle vary, Mark's being the longest since he included more of the details. The miracle took place right after Jesus' transfiguration. On that occasion the Father declared that Jesus was the well-beloved Son of God. Then strikingly, immediately after this heavenly approval of Jesus and His divine mission, He was confronted by the devil's angels.

A father came to Jesus for help. He gave Him a full description of his boy's symptoms and behavior when tormented by the demon (Mark 9:17–18, 21–22). Possibly, the boy suffered from epilepsy. This, however, in no way implies that all cases of this disease are caused by demon possession.

The disciples tried but failed to help the lad. When he was brought to Jesus, he had a seizure, causing him to have convulsions and foam at his mouth. The demon possession also left him mute. When the father affirmed his faith in Jesus, the Lord rebuked the demon, ordering him out of the boy. The demon obeyed Jesus' command, and the boy became so calm and relaxed that those who watched thought he had died (9:25–26).

There are other brief references to Jesus' exorcism of demons. Matthew referred to two, and Luke gave a parallel account of one that Matthew recorded (Matt. 9:32–34; 12:22–24; Luke 11:14–15).[5] In all three of these accounts Jesus cast out a demon from a man who could not speak. In one case Matthew added that the man was also blind (Matt. 12:22).

In addition, there are numerous references to demon exorcisms as a part of Jesus' miracle-working ministry among the people (Matt. 4:24; 8:16; Mark 1:32, 34; 16:9; Luke 4:41; 8:2; 13:32). Why, we might ask, was there so much apparent demonic activity and attendant exorcisms when Jesus was preaching? One of the most obvious reasons is that Jesus' message that the kingdom was at hand was understood by the demons of the kingdom of darkness and was taken seriously. John the Baptist, Jesus Himself, the twelve apostles, and the seventy who were sent out in pairs to preach, all proclaimed the same message to the people of Israel: "Repent for the kingdom of heaven is at hand."

As Konya explains, "The demon expulsions performed by Christ were not only seen as miracles, but they also demonstrated to His hearers that He was offering God's kingdom and that He was the Messiah-King. He came to destroy the works of Satan; and His triumph over the demonic realm proved He was who He claimed to be—the King and Conqueror, who came to offer that kingdom to Israel."[6]

There is a clear link between Jesus' casting out demons and His message about the kingdom of God which He said was "at hand." Frequently, when Jesus cast out a demon or demons, those close to the miracle recognized the supernatural at work. Not all, of course, saw it as God's supernatural power. Some, like the Pharisees, blasphemed the Spirit of God (by whose power Jesus performed His miracles), by saying that Jesus healed a blind, mute demon-possessed man by the power of Beelzebul (Matt. 12:24; Mark 3:22; Luke 11:19).

When Jesus and His representatives cast out demons and healed, they were invading Satan's kingdom. "In all of these instances, the casting out of demons served as a kind of preparation for the coming of the kingdom. Jesus' success, along with that of His representatives, showed that the time was near for Satan's dominion to end and for God to establish His kingdom on earth. These demonic expulsions were thus especially fitting to authenticate the message of the gospel of the kingdom preached by Jesus and His representatives."[7]

The kingdom message of Jesus and His servants included a contingency. Before the kingdom promised to David could be established, there had to be national repentance. But the leaders in Israel did not repent; only a believing remnant did. Because those acting for the nation did not meet the contingency, the kingdom was not established. So it will be established in the future when Jesus comes again to the earth and Israel is given a new heart in fulfillment of the New Covenant promised to her (Jer. 31:31–40; Ezek. 36:24–38; 37:21–28).

EXORCISMS PERFORMED BY THE APOSTLES

Jesus chose twelve men to be His apostles, His sent ones. These twelve were in a special sense the messengers or ambassadors of Jesus. They were His authorized representatives. They spoke and ministered in Jesus' name. One of the qualifications for the office of apostle was being an eyewitness of the risen Christ (Acts 1:15–26). Performing miracles confirmed the man and his message as an apostle (2 Cor. 12:12).

The ability to cast out demons was a sign that the one doing it was an apostle. Such work was described as a sign (Acts 5:12–16). Jesus gave His apostles whom He had chosen great abilities and authority. Among these was the healing of all kinds of sicknesses and diseases. Included in His descriptions of their assignment in this work was the ability to cast out demons. Jesus viewed exorcism of demons as a miracle-working power (Matt 10:1, 8; Mark 6:13; Luke 9:1).

The way in which the apostles cast out demons varied. Often they did it by a command in the name of Jesus (Mark 16:17; Acts 16:18). There is no recorded instance of delay in the actual deliverance from the demon. The miracle was immediate and definite. In one instance (Matt. 17:16; Mark 9:14–29; Luke 9:40) the apostles failed because believing prayer was needed in that difficult case. Today some who claim to cast out demons insist that some cases require a long period of time.

Philip the evangelist was closely associated with the apostles. They laid hands on him and those associated with him in ministry (Acts 6:6).

This meant the apostles were putting their blessing on the team and viewed them as partners in the work of the Lord. Philip, Luke wrote, was successful in casting out "unclean spirits" and "many who had been paralyzed and lame were healed" (8:7).

OTHER EXORCISMS IN THE NEW TESTAMENT

In addition to His twelve apostles, Jesus sent out "seventy others" (Luke 10:1) to go in pairs to prepare the way before Him. They were told to give the same message, "The kingdom of God has come near," and to have the same miracle-working power as that of the twelve apostles (10:9, 17).

After their tour of duty for the Master the seventy returned and reported to Him, "Lord, even the demons are subject to us in Your name" (10:17). Jesus responded by saying He was "watching Satan fall from heaven like lightning" (10:18). This was probably His way of describing how their power over demons and diseases was a successful confrontation of Satan's temporary rule. Or His words may have been a preview of Satan's fall in the Tribulation, which John mentioned in Revelation 12:9.

This miracle-working ability seems to have been a temporary assignment. We have no record that they continued healing the sick and casting out demons while Jesus was on earth.

When the Pharisees heard that Jesus healed a demon-possessed man who was blind and mute (Matt. 12:22), they could not deny the miracle; everyone could readily see the man had been healed. But the Pharisees said Jesus performed the miracle and cast out the demon "by Beelzebul the ruler of the demons" (12:24). Jesus responded, "And if I by Beelzebul cast out demons, by whom do your sons cast them out?" (10:27). Jesus' reference to "your sons" was doubtless to the Pharisees' disciples. Evangelicals differ over whether Jesus meant these Jewish exorcists actually cast demons out or that He was just going along with the Pharisees' belief that they did.[8]

If these "sons" of the Pharisees actually did cast out demons, they must have done so by Satan's power. Whatever they did was not the result of God's power working through them, because they were not rightly related to God through Jesus Christ.

Sceva's sons are called "exorcists" in Acts 19:13. They attempted to cast out demons but did not succeed. They even used the name of Jesus, but to no avail. Perhaps these men heard about Paul's work in Ephesus of casting out demons in Jesus' name. They tried to demand the demons leave people "by Jesus whom Paul preaches" (19:13), but it did not work.

The apostles were upset because they saw a man in their travels who was "casting out demons" (Mark 9:38) in Jesus' name. He was not one of the apostles, and Scripture gives no further identification of him. The apostles rebuked him, but Jesus did not side with what they did. Instead He indicated the man was not against Him but for Him (9:40) and that he would not speak evil of Jesus (9:39).

In Matthew 7:21–23 Jesus seems to have had in mind individuals like the Pharisees' sons, Sceva's sons, and others like them as He described those who claimed the right to enter His kingdom but would not be allowed to enter. "Not everyone who says to Me, 'Lord, Lord,' will enter the kingdom of heaven; but he who does the will of My Father who is in heaven. Many will say to Me on that day, 'Lord, Lord, did we not prophesy in Your name, and in Your Name cast out demons, and in Your name perform many miracles?' And then I will declare to them, 'I never knew you; depart from Me, you who practice lawlessness.'"

WHAT ABOUT EXORCISMS TODAY?

Many people today claim to know people who are or were demon-possessed, and many claim to have cast out demons. Do demons still take up residence in people? Do some have the ability to cast them out?

In New Testament times some people were indwelt by demons. As discussed earlier, I do not believe demons ever indwelt believers or do so now. The reason is that believers are God's people, His possession.

Do demons still possess some non-Christians? I see no reason to say they cannot, although Scripture gives no way to determine this. The devil is surely very active, probably still doing all the evil he ever did and more. His demons therefore continue their evil work too. While both believers and nonbelievers may be demon-*influenced* without being demon-possessed, the results of both may be similar, and we may not always be able to distinguish which it is.

What about exorcism today? Some extremely bizarre and radical behaviors accompany some of today's so-called exorcisms. A fifty-one-year-old Chicago woman called the police after she had been severely bruised and beaten by her husband and by a Presbyterian minister. Why had they abused her? They said they were trying to rid the woman of evil spirits.

In the Los Angeles area an even more horrifying experience occurred, purportedly in the name of Christianity. A group of preachers allegedly stomped a woman to death as they tried to remove demons from her. Also in San Francisco a woman, it was claimed, died as five people tried to exorcise demons from her, believing the demons were the source of her problems.[9]

Case after case could be cited of similar behaviors, all in the name of Jesus. Surely God is not pleased with such behavior. His name is not exalted and honored, regardless of how sincere the people involved may be.

Casting out demons in New Testament times was closely related to "gifts of healing" (lit., "gifts of healings," 1 Cor. 12:9). The Greek verb "to heal" is used in the Synoptics and Acts in association with casting out demons. Those from whom demons were cast out by Jesus and His apostles were said to be healed (Matt. 15:28; Luke 9:42; Acts 10:38). Konya writes, "Because of this, it is neither logical nor consistent with the New Testament pattern to separate the ability to cast out demons from the ability to heal miraculously the sick in general. Jesus, the Seventy (Luke 10:1, 17), the Eleven (Matt. 10:1; Acts 5:12), Philip (Acts 8:6–7) and Paul (Acts 19:11–12) were all able to heal the diseased and cast out demons." [10]

I do not believe anyone has the gift of healings today. Of course, God can and does heal, but the gift of healings was a sign gift, like that of the gift of tongues-speaking, given by the Holy Spirit to authenticate the apostles and their message (1 Cor. 14:22). So if the ability to cast out demons is still present, then so is the gift of healings. However, the sign gifts were already past for second-generation Christians (Heb. 2:3–4). [11]

It is bold and beyond our prerogative to demand that God or Satan do anything. It is far better for us to beseech God on the merit of Christ's finished work to grant deliverance from Satan and his cohorts. Rather than addressing demons directly, demanding that they leave a person, or speaking directly to Satan about anything—both risky practices—we should follow the advice of our Lord's half-brother James, "Submit therefore to God. Resist the devil and he will flee from you" (James 4:7).

SUMMARY

The New Testament records a number of instances of demon possession and of Jesus and His followers exorcising them. To be demon-possessed meant a demon or demons made his or their home in the person's physical body. Demon possession and demon influence must be distinguished; the former results in the work of a demon *within* an individual, whereas the latter describes a demon's work from *without*.

Because the Bible records no instances of believers being demon-possessed and because the Godhead would not share His residence with demons, I have argued that demons did not and do not indwell God's people today.

Demon possession manifested itself in physical and mental disorders. The person who was possessed usually experienced some mental derangement and often expressed physical violence. They were tormented. The New Testament does not specifically state the causes of demon possession, but idolatry and occultism do seem to be possible avenues for it. Since Satan and his demons are still active in the present age, unbelievers today may become demon-possessed.

Casting out demons is closely related to the miraculous sign gift of healings. Since these sign gifts were given to the apostles to authenticate them and their message about Jesus, the spiritual ability to exorcise demons may also have been a temporary gift no longer available today.

Saul Consults the Medium of Endor

"And Samuel said, 'Why then do you ask me, since the LORD has departed from you and has become your adversary? And the LORD has done accordingly as He spoke through me; for the LORD has torn the kingdom out of your hand and given it to your neighbor, to David.'"

(1 Sam. 28:16–17)

CHAPTER TWELVE
Spiritual Warfare—Man's Way and God's

THE REALITY OF SPIRITUAL WARFARE

WARFARE AMONG HUMANS is as old as the human race itself. Individuals, people groups, and nations have been waging battles with each other almost from the beginning of God's creation of humanity.

Spiritual warfare between Satan and God has persisted ever since Satan sinned. The conflict has centered in authority and control. The prideful desire to be like the Most High God was at the very heart of Satan's sin. Ever since he fell, Satan, together with his demons, has been in combat with God and His people. Satan still wants to be like the Most High God. Christians face a lifelong battle with Satan and his evil hosts. The war, however, has been won at Calvary and proof of that is the bodily resurrection of Christ. God's people are on the victory side.

In chapter 6 we noted that God's people are constantly opposed by the devil, their own sin nature, and the world. The Scriptures certainly do not hide the fact that believers are the target of satanic and demonic opposition. Spiritual warfare is real. God and Satan are not equals, both vying for authority in the world and over human beings. The triune God—Father, Son, and Holy Spirit—is absolutely sovereign, even over Satan. Satan is God's wicked supernatural foe opposing Him and battling for people's souls, but he is always subject to God.

SPIRITUAL WARFARE IN THE OLD TESTAMENT

In Old Testament times occult beliefs and practices were widespread. Entire communities of people lived in spiritual darkness and bondage and worshiped idols. The three cultures—Canaanite, Egyptian, and Babylonian—into which God placed the nation Israel were steeped in demonism with all its trappings. The Israelites, God's chosen people, were to be light in the midst of such spiritual darkness (Isa. 42:6). They often failed, as we do, to carry out their God-ordained commission.

David Powlison well summarizes the teaching of the Old Testament related to spiritual warfare. The Old Testament emphasizes that the true God is sovereign and is always at the center of the universe, never on the periphery. Humans are always seen as responsible for their actions whether good or evil. The Old Testament never blames Satan or demons for mankind's sinful behavior. The Old Testament does acknowledge the evil work of Satan and his demons, but it always presents God as sovereign and as circumscribing Satan and his work. In the Old Testament victory in the spiritual warfare is based on trusting in the Word and work of God, fearing Him, turning from evil, and resting in Him.[1]

What the Old Testament teaches about spiritual warfare contrasts strikingly with what "deliverance ministries" advocate. Although this is certainly not intentional, the spiritual warfare movement today has come perilously close to assuming God's prerogative and relegating Him to watching people bind Satan and confront the powers of evil. This is at least how their beliefs and practices appear. But this was never the case in the Old Testament. Satan is not God's equal; he is always subject to God, as are all the demons. This is a great comforting truth for the children of God.

SPIRITUAL WARFARE IN THE NEW TESTAMENT

Spiritual warfare, in other words, is not new. The New Testament has more to say about it than does the Old Testament. It repeatedly exhorts believers to beware of Satan's tactics and to equip themselves to oppose the devil. Paul warned the Corinthian Christians to be on guard for Satan's "schemes" (2 Cor. 2:11). He told the Ephesian Christians to "put on the full armor of God" so they could "stand firm against the schemes of the devil" (Eph. 6:10–11). James urged his readers to "resist the devil" (James 4:7). Peter, who experienced firsthand the devil's tricks, described how Satan, like a lion, is trying "to devour people" (1 Pet. 5:8).

CONTEMPORARY SPIRITUAL WARFARE MINISTRIES

Though spiritual warfare is not new, there is a renewed emphasis on it today. Entire ministries, in some instances, focus on human confrontation of evil powers and spiritual warfare, especially in relation to evangelism.

Some see three levels of spiritual warfare in which God's people need to be involved.[2] First is "ground-level spiritual warfare," which involves casting out demons from the possessed. The second level, "occult-level spiritual warfare," involves aggressively opposing in confrontational fashion stronger demonic powers which promote the occult. The third and highest level is "strategic-level spiritual warfare," which relates especially to evangelism and involves confronting territorial evil spirits directly. These demons are said to control entire geographical areas or people groups in their opposition to the gospel.

"Strategic-level spiritual warfare" is crucial to the spread of the gospel, it is believed.[3] This strategy includes "spiritual mapping," "identificational repentance," and "prophetic acts."[4] In "spiritual mapping" the demons' geographic area of activity is charted with the help of those who have special spiritual gifts to do this. Key demons are located by name. In "identificational repentance" believers confess the sins of groups of non-Christians, which keep them from receiving the gospel. "Prophetic acts" involve public opposition to and destruction of demonic devices, much as Old Testament prophets sometimes did.

Periods of Intensified Spiritual Warfare

Why is there such an elevated emphasis on the devil and his demons along with spiritual warfare today? I believe intensification of satanic activity today may well indicate that we are living in the last days of this present dispensation.

Satanic activity was especially prominent in other periods of biblical history. Satan's challenge of God's right to rule, of course, began with his own fall. Then he challenged our first parents to become like God. Just before the Exodus Satan confronted God through Pharaoh and the gods of Egypt. Throughout Israel's history Satan opposed God by getting His people to bow before idols even when they were in the Promised Land. Satan and the demons of hell were extremely active during the life and ministry of Christ on earth. The early life and times of the church were marked by persecution inspired by Satan and the martyrdom of many of God's people. In the future, during the coming Great Tribulation, the seventieth week of Daniel, Satan will again pour out his hatred of God and His people in unprecedented ways.

Reasons for Intensified Spiritual Warfare Today

Terry C. Hulbert lists ten factors he feels have contributed to the spiritual warfare emphasis today.

1. A decrease in knowledge of and respect for the Bible. Many evangelicals know little of what the Bible teaches (as Barna's research reveals) and do not take its standards seriously. [George Barna's research, reported in his book, *What Americans Believe,* showed that almost half the evangelicals in the United States deny the existence of Satan, seeing him only as a symbol of all that is evil.]
2. A diminishing of the importance of biblical values among believers as determinative for belief and behavior, thus leaving them vulnerable to Satan's temptations.
3. The increased immigration of people who bring with them a variety of nonbiblical (satanic) religions as evidenced by the increasing number of [Muslim] mosques and Hindu temples.
4. A trend toward pluralism, the relativistic, nonjudgmental attitude that denies absolutes and accepts contrabiblical beliefs as valid.
5. The secularization and trivialization of the events of the birth, death, and resurrection of Christ, and a mythologizing of God and Satan. The former detracts from the deity of Christ and the supreme significance of his life and work; the latter makes man

himself the ultimate reality and deceives him by implying that he can control his own destiny in this life and after death.

6. An increased acceptance of a humanistic perspective in psychology and counseling and in popular attitudes which ignore the reality of God and the fact of sin.

7. An increased fascination and involvement with the occult, horoscopes, and New Age concepts and practices.

8. An increase in the sense of spiritual vacuum and loss of control resulting from secularism and humanism, which leads many to turn to occult practices.

9. The influence of recent literature, some speculative, some deceptive, which constitutes both a cause and an effect. In some cases the result has been positive, raising the level of awareness of satanic activity. The media, especially some movies, television programs, and music videos have also contributed to this trend.

10. The denial of sin as man's basic problem. Sin is essentially submission to Satan and rebellion against God, as it was in the beginning with Adam and Eve.[5]

SPIRITUAL WARFARE AND
THE SPREAD OF THE GOSPEL

Territorial Spirits

Do "territorial spirits" control certain geographic areas and places, and must they be named, confronted, and cast out before the gospel can be effective in that locale? C. Peter Wagner answers yes. "The hypothesis I am suggesting, then, is that . . . Satan delegates high ranking members of the hierarchy of evil spirits to control nations, regions, cities, tribes, people groups, neighborhoods and other significant social networks of human beings throughout the world. Their major assignment is to prevent God from being glorified in their territory, which they do through directing the activity of lower ranking demons."[6]

Wagner then referred to some missionaries who were not able to live or minister until they drove out the demons there: "The missionaries finally took seriously the demonic occupation of that geographical spot, engaged the demons in a power encounter and drove them out."[7]

Identifying the demons by name is also a part of driving them out of an area and thus supposedly making it possible for the gospel to be effective there.

Nowhere does the Bible teach that demons are assigned to geographic areas. Daniel did speak of the evil "prince of Persia" and the evil "prince of Greece" (Dan. 10:13, 20). In these instances supernatural creatures apparently attempted to manipulate the human rulers of these areas. But are we to assume from this that demons were actually rulers of these areas and that all regions of the world are thus dominated by demon rulers today who can be named and driven out by man? This assumption seems to go beyond what the Scriptures state. The apostle Paul did not associate the powers of darkness with any specific country or geographic area.[8] Neither did he ever engage in the type of spiritual warfare embraced by the "deliverance ministries" so popular today.

Binding Satan

Do believers have the power and responsibility to "bind Satan" and thus to free the Spirit of God to work through God's Word in evangelism? Those carrying on "deliverance ministries" and engaged in "confronting the powers" believe so. Ed Murphy puts it this way: "The experienced deliverance minister can compel evil spirits to tell the truth. I do so all the time. . . . *To evangelize the demonized we must learn how to bind demonic activity from the minds of demonized unbelievers.*"[9] I do not find such an assignment for the child of God anywhere in the Bible.

None of the passages so often used to support the alleged practice of binding Satan and demons and delivering the "demonized" say what the "deliverance ministers" claim them say. Of course, Satan is the believer's enemy and he opposes believers (1 Thess. 2:18). Yes, Satan is "the ruler of this world," "the god of this world," and "the prince of the power of the air" (John 12:31; 14:30; 16:11; 2 Cor. 4:4; Eph. 2:2). No Bible believer denies that the twelve apostles and the seventy were given miraculous sign gifts, including the ability to cast out demons (Matt. 10:1; Luke 10:17).

Does this mean God's ministers have that same ability today? The apostles were also able to raise the dead (Matt. 10:8). Certainly that ability is not available today. How then can "deliverance ministers" say they have the same abilities as the apostles?

No one of the Scriptures used by these people in defense of what they do in deliverance ministries supports their work. The Bible never calls on us to name the demons, discover the reason for the demonization, and demand Satan and the demons to leave. Nowhere are these activities required to enable God to act. Evangelism, instead, comes by the Spirit of God using the Word of God.

We should reject any ministry that does not believe the gospel alone is "the power of God for salvation to everyone who believes" (Rom. 1:16). Speaking of their "authority in Christ," deliverance enthusiasts state that when a severely demonized person comes to faith in Christ, there is "no guarantee that *all* of the demons . . . will immediately release their hold on the new believer."[10] No, God the Holy Spirit does not need the help of a "deliverance minister" to complete what He began.

Those who say believers are to "bind" Satan appeal to three usages of the word "bind" in Matthew (12:29; 16:19; 18:18). When Jesus spoke of binding a strong man before a thief could plunder his house (12:29), He was responding to the religious leaders who had accused Him of casting out demons in the power of Satan, the prince of demons. His point was that by driving out demons, He was proving He is greater than Satan. "He was able to go into Satan's realm . . . [the 'strong man's house'], the demonic world, and come away with the spoils of victory."[11] But nothing in the passage suggests that believers can bind Satan. In fact, this statement by Jesus may have been given in anticipation of Satan being bound for the duration of the thousand-year Millennium (Rev. 20:1–3).

Our Lord told Peter, "Whatever you shall bind on earth shall be bound in heaven, and whatever you shall loose on earth shall be loosed in heaven" (Matt. 16:19). Many overlook the fact that Jesus said essentially the same thing to the other apostles (18:18). The apostles certainly understood the terminology their Master used to mean that they would have the authority to tell people on earth what God had already decided in heaven. Jesus told them this in view of their opportunity and responsibility to take the message of salvation to the Gentiles. What God has said in heaven—salvation is by faith in Christ—was the message they were to declare on earth. This is precisely what they did, with Peter leading the way, in the house of Cornelius (Acts 10).

SPIRITUAL WARFARE GOD'S WAY

Proponents of a "deliverance ministry," or as Powlison calls it, the "ekballistic mode of ministry,"[12] claim biblical support for their view. They appeal to the Synoptic Gospels (Matthew, Mark, and Luke) and Acts. These books show a dramatic, drastic change from the Old Testament's lack of emphasis on demonic indwelling and expulsion. These books record unusual satanic activity as Christ invaded the demons' domain and as the church was born. We see a similar kind of shift from the Book of Acts to Romans and the rest of the New Testament.

The Epistles give much attention to Satan and his evil cohorts, but they do not include any exhortation or instruction to cast out demons. Neither the Epistles, nor the Synoptics, nor Acts teach that satanic and demonic attacks on the believers result necessarily from believers' sin.

"Deliverance ministries" usually stress the evil work of demons and their need to be cast out, whereas Scripture places the blame not on the demons but on individuals' sins, such as evil speaking, backbiting, unbelief, lack of love, thanklessness, lust, and a host of other such sins. No biblical support exists for saying these sins are caused by demons— "a demon of lust" or "a demon of envy," for example. Instead Christians are responsible for their sins, and they need to confess them and with God's help to forsake them. In other words, God places the responsibility for the sinful behavior not on Satan or his demons but on believers themselves.

As previously discussed, each believer has three enemies—the devil, the world, and the flesh. The way of victory, however, is not deliverance or escape from these enemies in this life but constant opposition to them in the power of the Spirit of God. Christians are to "stand" against Satan, to "resist" him, to "love not the world (KJV)," and not to let sin reign in their mortal bodies (Eph. 6:14; James 4:7; 1 John 2:15; Rom. 6:12).

The Bible gives many clear commands to believers on how they are to wage battle against Satan and his demons. We have already referred to many of these commands as we have discussed other topics in this study. I have chosen to highlight one of those commands here even though it has been introduced earlier.

Each of the three passages highlighted below tells us to do the same thing—to oppose Satan. When we oppose him, of course, we are opposing his demons as well, for they engage in the same work.

It is important to note how different, even contrary, this basic command is to what the "deliverance ministry" enthusiasts preach. God's way for His children to engage in spiritual warfare with the enemy of their souls finds no parallel with much of what is preached and practiced today.

Ephesians 6:10–20

Resisting the devil, Paul explained, is done by putting on the "full armor of God" (Eph. 6:13). Only when equipped with this armor can we "stand firm against the schemes of the devil" and "spiritual forces of wickedness in the heavenly places." Putting on the armor, Paul wrote, can enable us to "resist in the evil day" (6:13).

As noted earlier, the armor to be put on here is Christ in the sense that each of the pieces represents Him. He is put on by faith at the time of salvation. This places the believing sinner in Christ. What Paul called for in Ephesians 6 was not the salvation of his readers but the appropriation by faith of all they have in Christ. That Christ Himself is the armor is affirmed in Romans 13:14, where Paul told the Roman Christians the same thing he told the Ephesian believers: "Put on the Lord Jesus Christ, and make no provision for the flesh in regard to its lusts."

James 4:7–10

James, our Lord's half-brother, wrote to Christian Jews, many of whom had been dispersed from their homeland. While Paul (Eph. 6:10–20) and Peter (1 Pet. 5:8–9) linked the devil with the believer's trials and sufferings, James wrote of the devil in relation to a believer's own sinfulness.

The devil can gain a "foothold" (Eph. 4:27 NIV) in our lives when we flirt with and fool with sin.

Before James's exhortation in James 4:7–10 to resist the devil, he mentioned a number of sins God's people are often guilty of, such as self-claimed wisdom, doubting God, double-mindedness, hearing but not doing God's Word, a loose tongue, pride, and others. James blamed these sins not on Satan or demons but on the believers themselves.

These four verses in James 4 include ten commands. In Greek, each one is an aorist imperative, stressing the need for decisive action on the part of believers. The command to "resist the devil" follows the command to "submit therefore to God' (4:7). "Submit" is a military term meaning to be subordinated, that is, to give obedience to one's superior. This is the positive side. The negative side is to "resist," that is, stand against or oppose the devil. When believers carry out their responsibilities, God promises that the devil "will flee from you."

Verses 7 and 8 present two comforting promises. When a child of God takes a stand against the devil, Satan flees. And when a believer draws near to God, God does not flee, but in response He draws near to that believer (4:8).

Believers have no authority to rebuke the devil, to bind Satan, or to even talk to him. However, they do have the charge to resist him, and this can only be done after they have drawn near to God. How can a Christian draw near to God? By believing and obeying His Word. How can a Christian resist the devil? The same way Jesus did—by using the Word of God. Our Lord responded to Satan's temptation of Him and Satan's misuse of Scripture by affirming it correctly. We, too, have the Word of God as our defensive weapon. Satan hates God's Word just as much as he hates God Himself.

First Peter 5:8–9

Peter wrote his first epistle to suffering saints scattered throughout Asia Minor away from their homeland and in hostile environments. His aim was to encourage these people in their faith and to help them live above all the ridicule and reproach they were experiencing. He instructed them to be faithful to God and to care for fellow believers. When Peter wrote that Christians are to "resist" the devil, he used the word Paul and James used (Eph. 6:13; James 4:7).

Again, Peter's call to resist Satan is accompanied by a positive command to cast "all your anxiety upon Him, because He cares for you" (1 Pet. 5:7). When we do this, we are better prepared to resist the devil. Our archenemy stalks about like a lion seeking out his next victim, not roaring all the time but hiding his true identity and aim until he sees the opportune moment to pounce on his prey. Like a lion, Satan is subtle and powerful.

The command is to "resist him, firm in your faith" (5:9). As in Ephesians 6 and James 4, so here there is no call to bind Satan or even to speak to him, but to stand against him. This, Peter said, is to be done in and through our faith, that is, just as we trusted Christ for salvation, so we are to exercise faith in Him each day.

Obeying this clear command to resist the devil is the responsibility of each believer as he or she engages in spiritual warfare. Obedience to commands of Scripture such as this brings divine deliverance. This is God's way for His children as they engage in spiritual warfare.

SUMMARY

Each one of us must "resist the devil" personally. No one can do it for us, not even someone engaged in so-called deliverance ministry. We cannot do it for someone else. We need not learn the names of demons harassing us or others. Nor can we bind Satan, for no such authority has ever been given to us. Even Jesus did not bind Satan when he tempted Him to sin. Satan is a defeated foe and so are his demons. His and their defeat was accomplished at Calvary. It is not God's will that Satan be bound now. But he will be bound for the one thousand years of Christ's millennial reign (Rev. 20:1–3). Afterward, he will be released for a short time and then will be thrown into the lake of fire prepared for him and his angels (20:7–10).

Peter Delivered from Prison

"And behold, an angel of the Lord suddenly appeared, and a light shone in the cell; and he struck Peter's side and roused him, saying, 'Get up quickly.' And his chains fell off his hands. And the angel said to him, 'Gird yourself and put on your sandals.' And he did so. And he said to him, 'Wrap your cloak around you and follow me.' And he went out and continued to follow, and he did not know that what was being done by the angel was real, but thought he was seeing a vision." (Acts 12:7–9)

CHAPTER THIRTEEN
Commonly Asked Questions about Angels and Demons

⸻⸺⸻

S OME QUESTIONS ABOUT ANGELS and demons have been asked repeatedly for a long time. Other questions are rather new and have surfaced because of the increased interest in angels. In other words, what Duane Garrett calls "Angelphilia"—"current extensive interest in and even devotion to angels"—has given rise to new questions.

This chapter raises some of these old and new questions and seeks to provide answers from the Scriptures. Some of these questions have already been answered earlier in our discussion. In cases where an issue has already been discussed, we will not go over the material again. Here, however, we want to discuss twenty-three questions.

Perhaps the most difficult problem in answering the many questions often asked about angels and demons is how to know whether they are still doing today the things they did in Bible times. Because angels did certain things to certain people at certain times in the Bible does not necessarily mean they do those things now. In other words, the issue of the close of the canon of Scripture and the doctrine of the progress of revelation enter the picture. Many things recorded in Scripture are not going on today. God works differently with different people in different time periods. And for that we ought to be thankful. Are you not glad, for example, that we do not get stoned today for picking up sticks on Saturday, as was the case under the Mosaic Law (Num. 15:32–36)? The fact that something is recorded in the Bible does not in itself mean it is in effect today.

The questions we raise and attempt to answer here will serve as a review and summary of a number of points already discussed in this book. No special significance is intended by the order in which the questions are set forth.

IS CHRISTIANITY THE ONLY RELIGION THAT INCLUDES BELIEF IN ANGELS?

No, Christianity is not the only world religion that incorporates angels in its beliefs. Judaism and Islam, for example, include belief in angels in their systems.

DID GOD CREATE ANGELS IN HIS IMAGE?

Some evangelicals believe God created angels in His own image and after His likeness, just as He created man. C. Fred Dickason, for example, says that the image of God consists of personality and holiness. Since angels have both of these, they were created in His image.[1] However, two facts speak against this view.

First, the Bible does not say they were created in the image of God. Second, the image of God in mankind means more than personality and holiness. It also relates to having dominion over the earth. Angels do not have this, but people do. The image of God also relates to knowledge, holiness, and righteousness restored in Jesus Christ (Eph. 4:22–25; Col. 3:9–10).[2]

HOW MUCH DO ANGELS KNOW ABOUT GOD'S PLAN AND OUR LIVES?

Scripture is silent about this. That is, the Bible has no specific statement telling us what they know and do not know. Of course, we can be sure they are not omniscient, because only God has complete knowledge of all things. On the other hand, angels are greater in power (and presumably in knowledge) than people. In the Bible we learn about angelic ministry to humans on many occasions. We can assume from this that they must know of human needs and whereabouts in order to minister to them. Satan and his demons are set forth in the Bible as deceptive schemers. It may follow therefore that they know more about us than we wish they did; otherwise how could they deceive?

Based on the whole teaching of Scripture concerning angels, it seems fair to say angels—both good and bad—have far more knowledge about many things than we do but far less than God does.

IS JESUS AN ANGEL?

Jesus the Son of God is most certainly not an angel. All angels are creatures; He is the Creator (John 1:1–3; Col. 1:16–17; Heb. 1:2). The Lord Jesus Christ is superior to any of the angels. He is the Son of God in a unique sense. Bible references to Christ's Sonship speak of His divine essence, reflecting His equality with God.

Perhaps the idea of Jesus being the "King of angels" comes from the fact that artists often have drawn a halo around His head. Angels are sometimes presented that way too. "Perhaps those artists had encountered angels as luminescent light beings and couldn't quite come up with a way of painting them properly. Halos evolved to represent the golden light that observers had seen shining from the face of angels."[3]

Jesus never was an angel, is not now an angel, nor will He ever become an angel. The thought that the Son of God was or is an angel comes not from the Bible but from the second-century Gnostic heresy, which was soundly condemned by the church fathers of the early centuries.

SHOULD WE WORSHIP ANGELS?

Nowhere in Scripture are people told to worship angels. Instead, God's Word exhorts us *not* to pay homage to them (Rev. 22:8–9). Worship of angels is condemned in Paul's letter to the Colossians (Col. 2:18). At the time he wrote, the people of Colossae were steeped in the cult of angel worship. Angels were viewed as mediators between God and man. Angels were even thought to control the elements of the world. Such sin distracted from the supremacy and centrality of Christ, and has always done so. In our own day we are seeing a similar kind of angel cult.

SHOULD WE PRAY TO ANGELS?

The Bible teaches that God's people are to address God the Father in prayer in the name of God the Son and in the power of the Holy Spirit. There is absolutely no Scripture that instructs anyone to pray to angels.

In the history of the church many have prayed to angels, however. Some do today. Books on angels often encourage readers to pray to angels for protection, guidance, healing, and rescue from danger. Pope Pius XI (1922–39) is said to have prayed twice every day to his angel. Pope John XXIII (1958–63) admitted he did the same, especially asking his guardian angel to help him as he carried out his work. Regardless of who has done it or who does it today, praying to angels is not scriptural.

WILL WE BECOME ANGELS IN HEAVEN?

Because believers will have "heavenly bodies" (1 Cor. 15:40) as do angels, we will be *like* angels. We will also be like them in that we will render ceaseless praise and worship to God.

However, angels can never experience salvation by God's grace. In heaven Christians will have glorified bodies. But holy angels have never been glorified because they have never sinned. In the resurrection believers will become *like* angels to some degree (Matt. 22:30), but they will never actually *become* angels.

It is not uncommon at a funeral service, especially at one of a baby or a young child, to hear someone say of the deceased, "Now he (or she) is an angel." Is this true? Do people become angels when they die? No, the Bible always keeps humans and angels distinct. This is true of humans both before and after death. Angels do not die and they do not reproduce. The Bible makes no mention of baby angels; all angels were created individually at the same time.

DO ANGELS AGE AND DIE?

When God created humans, He created man and then from his side He created woman. The two were told to "be fruitful and multiply, and fill the earth" (Gen. 1:28). God did not create a pair of angels and equip them with powers of reproduction. Instead, He created them all at the same time. They exist as an order of creation.

Since angels are deathless (Luke 20:36) and do not reproduce after their kind (Matt. 22:30), the number of angels in existence now is the same as the number when God created them. There are no baby angels, so there are no more angels now than there ever were.

DO ANGELS HAVE GENDER?

Angels are always referred to in the Bible as masculine, with one possible exception (Zech. 5:9). However, the cherubim in Ezekiel 1 had faces like lions and eagles. Christ the Son of God appears in Revelation 5:6 as "a Lamb standing, as if slain, having seven horns and seven eyes." Could it be that all such descriptions are symbolic representations for the reader's benefit and not declarations of who angels and Christ really are? Garrett writes:

> The fact remains that we know nothing about angel gender. Speculation can seriously mislead us here. Belief that angels are both male and female can lead to the bizarre notions of angelic reproduction and emanations that we have seen in Gnosticism and paganism, and it is the doorway to angelic mythology.
>
> On the other hand, belief that angels are androgynous beings is also unsatisfactory. It leads to the kind of art that portrays angels as effeminate males. As humans, we can only react with revulsion to such a being. We relate to visual images and ascribe value to them within our own earthly, human frame of reference. We might see strength, courage, and justice in a virile man or grace and compassion in a beautiful woman. But we see only a monstrosity in a hermaphrodite.
>
> Therefore, I think we would be better off to understand angels as neither male nor female nor androgynous but simply as sexless. They are beings for whom gender has no meaning.[4]

DO ANGELS HAVE WINGS?

Some angels do have wings. At least the ones Isaiah saw in his vision had wings (Isa. 6). In fact, the seraphim each had three pairs of wings. One pair covered each angel's face, one pair the feet, and with the third pair each angel flew (6:2). The cherubim Ezekiel saw had four wings each (Ezek. 1:11). The fact that the angel Gabriel went to Daniel "in swift flight" (Dan. 9:21 NIV) suggests that Gabriel has wings. The same is true of an angel whom the apostle John saw "flying in midair" (Rev. 14:6 NIV).

Does this mean all angels have wings? Not necessarily, though they may have. Whether all angels have or do not have wings, they can and do carry out God's bidding swiftly. They are never late in fulfilling an assignment.

DOES EVERYONE HAVE A GUARDIAN ANGEL?

Many today who do not pretend to base their beliefs about angels on the Bible do believe that everyone—Christian and non-Christian—has at least one guardian angel. Some even advocate that animals and trees have guardian angels. Not too strangely, these same advocates never say anything about these guardian angels disciplining the ones they guard.

The Bible does not use the term "guardian angels." True, a number of early Christian writers did affirm belief in guardian angels. Later, classic theologians did the same. Origen and Thomas Aquinas, for example, both sought to defend the belief in guardian angels. While all this is, of course, significant, it does not prove that each person has one or more specific angels watching over him or her.

Sophy Burnham, in her book *Angel Letters*, gives many testimonies from people claiming firsthand contact with and ministry from their guardian angels. Their angels warned them of imminent danger, helped them change a tire, healed the sick, and brought peace to the dying. People from various religious faiths and some with none give their testimonies. Guardian angels, they say, are nonjudgmental; they just love and care for those to whom they are assigned.

What does the Bible teach about guardian angels? As stated above, it nowhere refers to them by using the word "guardian." This does not mean that guardian angels do not exist. The question is not whether holy angels minister to God's people. Indeed they do. Rather, the question is, Does everyone—believers and unbelievers—have one or more angels?

Two passages of Scripture relate directly to the question at hand. Hebrews 1:14 clearly reveals that the principal function of holy angels in relation to Christians is service. "Are they not all ministering spirits, sent out to render service for the sake of those who will inherit salvation?" First and foremost the service is to God on behalf of those "who shall be heirs of salvation." This would include all who come to faith in Christ. When does this ministry begin? It would seem natural for it to begin as soon as life begins and continue on through life on earth. We have no hint from this verse whether one or more angels are assigned to carry out this ministry.

The second passage bearing on this subject is Matthew 18:10. With specific reference to infants and growing children, Jesus said, "See that you do not despise one of these little ones, for I say to you, that their angels in heaven continually behold the face of My Father who is in heaven." Some believe holy angels perform a general ministry on behalf of God's children, while others believe this passage teaches that each child as well as each Christian has a specific angel serving as his or her guardian.

When people concentrate on their supposed guardian angels, they inevitably get their eyes away from God. Their angel replaces God. Also, overemphasis on one's guardian angel makes it easy to pray to that angel instead of to God.

CAN PEOPLE CONTACT ANGELS TODAY?

Here is how one contemporary writer caught up in angelmania answers this question.

> People talk to themselves, their pets and their plants, so why not to their angels? By all accounts, angels do listen, so you'd be wise to communicate your needs to them, especially during a crisis.
>
> In the aftermath of a terrible highway accident, a woman named Marlene huddled in the wreckage of her car, trying to calm her daughter, Victoria. She remembers praying to her guardian angel for help. Rescue

workers arrived almost immediately and one firefighter reached in through the smashed window to give her daughter a teddy bear, her favorite toy. Victoria stopped crying and cuddled the bear while the firefighters freed her and her mother.

Later that week, Marlene and Victoria visited the fire station to thank the firefighters for their help and for the teddy bear. But the firefighters were just a little puzzled. They never carried stuffed animals and had never given one to anyone at an accident.

You can talk to your angels out loud or in your minds, whatever feels comfortable for you. Either way, they'll hear you.[5]

Tradition says fifteenth century Joan of Arc was visited by an angel, who told her to lead the French Army to victory. Some people today say the angels they see are cloudlike formations. Others say they appear as balls of energy and some even describe them as intense white fog. Sometimes, we are told, angels contact people in dreams to give life-saving instruction.

Angels did contact individuals in the Bible. What they said and did is recorded as part of the Word of God. But we have no instruction to seek contact with angels today. God's revelation in Scripture is complete. The only supernatural Being we are enjoined to contact is God the Father through God the Son in the power of God the Holy Spirit. Furthermore, angels do not need people to contact them. They get their orders from God, not from us.

DO ANGELS EAT AND SLEEP?

Angels do not have physical bodies so they do not need to eat. And yet two of them did eat a meal with Abraham and Sarah in their tent "by the oaks of Mamre" (Gen. 18:1–2). They are identified as angels in Genesis 19:1.

These two angels looked like men, but they were really angels. They announced to Abraham that his wife Sarah would have a son even though she was beyond child-bearing age and Abraham was very old as well. Sarah laughed at the announcement the angels made. Later, however, Isaac was born. His name means "he laughs."

This was a most unusual experience. It remains true that angels have no need to eat food.

Angels do not need sleep either, and this is for the same reason that they do not need food—they are spirit beings. Classic and contemporary literature and art often erroneously picture angels as sleeping on soft clouds.[6]

IS THERE A RELATIONSHIP BETWEEN
ANGELS AND STARS?

The question of the relationship between angels and stars has been pursued from earliest times. Some fanciful and far-fetched views have been advanced. The Bible does seem to relate angels to stars, but it also keeps them distinct.

Many times when the Hebrew word for stars is used, the Old Testament writers implied that they are more than astronomical entities. They speak of stars in more personal ways; the stars are said to fight, sing, and even err (Judg. 5:20; Job 15:15; 25:5; 38:7; Ps. 148:3).

Also the New Testament gives evidence of some relationship between stars and angels. The Greek word for stars often denotes or symbolizes a personal entity (e.g., 1 Cor. 15:35–45; Jude 13) and not just a heavenly luminary. Christ Himself is called "the morning star" (2 Pet. 1:19; Rev. 22:16). The "star" that led the Magi to the Christ child is believed by some to be the Shekinah glory of God, thereby indicating that the Lord Himself was present among men.[7]

What then is the relationship between angels and stars? James Woychuck's summary seems to fit the biblical picture.

> Biblical testimony does not remove all the mystery from the connection between the stars and angels. The exact relationship of stars and angels may be inconceivable and inexpressible this side of heaven. But God's Word does reveal that, by God's design, the countless millions of stars visually portray the countless millions of angels. Further, this portrayal extends to depict a presently indefinable intersection in the being of stars and angels. Therefore, the stars do not merely offer an illustration of the innumerable and powerful angels but also portray God's vast armies of light intentionally, creatively, and universally. When people look up on a twinkling gust of shining diamonds too

numerous to count, they see the visual representation of the angels. They see stars and yet, in a mysterious way, they see something more.[8]

WHO WERE THE ANGELS IN REVELATION 2 AND 3?

John addressed "the angel" of seven churches in Asia Minor. Who were these angels? As noted earlier, the Greek word for "angel" means "messenger." It is used most often of spirit beings but also of humans at times (e.g., Mark 1:3; Luke 7:24; 9:52; James 2:25).

In each of the seven occurrences in Revelation 2 and 3 the word is in the singular. Since Scripture nowhere else suggests that an angel is assigned to each local church, it seems best to see these messengers as referring to the pastor of each church.[9] Furthermore, it is difficult to conceive of the Spirit of God instructing spirit beings to direct the affairs of a local church.

WHY DOES GOD ALLOW
SATAN AND DEMONS TO EXIST?

To ask this question another way, Why did God not send Satan and the angels who followed him in his rebellion against God to the lake of fire immediately after they sinned?

We could ask a similar question with regard to the human race. Why did God not wipe out Adam and Eve when they sinned? Why does God not bring us sudden death when we sin? The only answer to such questions is that His grace withstands His judgment.

When God chose to allow evil to come into the world, He chose the best possible plan to bring the most possible glory to Himself. God uses what He allows the devil and his demons to do to teach us the graces we need for maturity in Christ. When we cling to Him, He sees us through the toughest battles Satan can wage. We can triumph in Christ.

DO DEMONS CAUSE US TO SIN?

The devil (and doubtless his demons) tempt God's people to sin. But there is no teaching in the Bible that the devil and demons *cause* people to sin.

James wrote that the cause of our sin is not God, for He does not tempt anyone to evil (James 1:13). What then is the source of temptation and eventual sin? "But each one is tempted when he is carried away and enticed by his own lust. Then when lust has conceived, it gives birth to sin; and when sin is accomplished, it brings forth death" (1:14–15). The devil and demons do not make us do anything, and that includes sin. We choose to sin just as surely as we choose not to sin.

HOW CAN WE KNOW WHEN WE ARE BEING OPPOSED BY SATAN AND/OR DEMONS?

The Bible is clear that Christians are the objects of Satan's and his demons' attacks. We are not told, however, how we are to distinguish between their opposition and the conflicts and difficulties we bring on ourselves. In other words, there are times when we are reaping the results of poor or bad decisions and Satan and his demons may not be involved.

It is best, therefore, for us to evaluate our own behavior before blaming Satan and demons for every obstacle and problem we face. When we discover that we ourselves are the cause of a problem, we should take definite steps not to repeat past mistakes or sins. If God's Spirit convinces us we are being assaulted by Satan and demons, we need to remind ourselves of the armor of Ephesians 6, which God has provided for us. In the strength of God's Spirit we then can resist Satan and claim victory in Christ.

CAN A CHRISTIAN BE POSSESSED BY DEMONS?

As we noted earlier, students of the Scriptures answer this question differently. Some are sure that Christians can be and sometimes are possessed by demons. Others are just as sure that Christians cannot be possessed by demons, though they may be attacked and afflicted by them. The reason for this difference of opinion is that the Bible does not address the question specifically.

To arrive at an acceptable answer, we must understand the difference between demon possession and demonic influence. When demons possess someone, they take up residence inside that person. This is far more than the evil influence of demons on God's people, which is constant and will continue until the believer is in heaven. Demon possession is an internal attack, while demonic influence involves external attacks.

Two related scriptural truths help answer this question. First, since God the Holy Spirit permanently indwells every believer, would He share His residence with the demons of hell? Second, do the Scriptures record any indisputable cases of demons possessing believers? When these questions are answered in harmony with God's Word, the answer to the original question must be "No, people who have been born again cannot be possessed by demons."

DO CHRISTIANS TODAY HAVE POWER TO CAST OUT DEMONS?

Again, Bible-believing Christians answer this question differently. Some answer yes and others say no. What does the Bible say? God's Word does tell us that Jesus sent out His apostles and the seventy and gave them power to cast out demons and heal all kinds of diseases (Matt. 10:1, 8), and they were very successful in doing just that.

Does this mean God's people today have that same power and authority? I think not and here is why. The ministry our Lord gave to the apostles and the seventy was a special, temporary arrangement. He sent them out to announce to the nation Israel that individuals needed to repent—that is, to change their minds about Jesus the Messiah, about themselves, and about their sin—before He would institute His kingdom on earth. To authenticate themselves as genuine representatives of the Messiah and their message, they were given miracle-working power. Decades later, when the Scriptures were completed, God's messengers no longer needed the sign gifts the apostles and others possessed. We now have God's written Word as our authentication.

WILL THERE EVER BE ANOTHER FALL OF HOLY ANGELS?

The angels had a probationary period, as did our first parents. Both Adam and Eve and a large number of angels (including Lucifer) failed the test

God put before them. Has there ever been a time since then when angels fell? And will there ever be a time in the future when more holy angels might rebel against God?

The Bible does not address this issue directly. But the Bible's silence on the matter suggests no other fall of angels has occurred in the past or will occur in the future.

WHAT ABOUT SAUL AND THE MEDIUM AT ENDOR?

The Philistines had their army all set to fight against the Israelites. They were stationed at a place called Shunem (1 Sam. 28:4). This was located several miles east of Megiddo and gave them easy access to the plain of Jezreel where the battle was to be waged. When Saul realized what his army faced, he panicked.

As many of us do in times of danger, Saul cried out to God—but he got no answer. So he told one of his servants to "seek for me a woman who is a medium, that I may go to her and inquire of her" (28:7). This is quite surprising because before this incident, Saul had already ordered all the "mediums and spiritists" removed from the land (28:3). This was in accord with God's clear command in Deuteronomy 18:10–11: "There shall not be found among you anyone who makes his son or his daughter pass through the fire, one who uses divination, one who practices witchcraft, or one who interprets omens, or a sorcerer, or one who casts a spell, or a medium, or a spiritist, or one who calls up the dead."

Saul's servant found a medium who had somehow escaped Saul's attempts to rid the land of spiritists. A medium was one who practiced necromancy, communicating with the dead to find out what the future would bring. This particular medium was still hiding out at Endor. When she was brought to Saul, he disguised himself so she would not recognize him.

Saul asked the medium to bring Samuel up from the dead (1 Sam. 28:11). She did as Saul asked her to do and Samuel came back from the dead. Presumably she did not expect this to happen, because when she saw him, she "cried out with a loud voice" (28:12).

Charles Ryrie's summary of this experience is an excellent explanation of what happened. "On this occasion, God miraculously permitted the actual spirit of Samuel to speak and announce Saul's imminent death (v. 19). The medium's cry of astonishment shows that this appearance was not the result of her usual tricks."[10]

DO ANGELS SHARE THE GOSPEL?

No, angels do not share the gospel of God's saving grace with humans, for they were never assigned this task. It is the task of God's redeemed people to give the message of salvation to those who have not yet been delivered from sin's shackles. Christians are the God-appointed ambassadors for Christ (2 Cor. 5:20).

If even a small portion of the attention given to angels, Satan, and demons today would be given to the spread of the gospel, we would see many more delivered from Satan's stronghold and entering the family of God.

Joseph Is Warned to Flee into Egypt

"But when Herod was dead, behold an angel of the Lord appeared in a dream to Joseph in Egypt, saying, 'Arise and take the Child and His mother, and go into the land of Israel; for those who sought the Child's life are dead.'" (Matt. 2:19–20)

CHAPTER FOURTEEN
How Shall We Then Live?

⚬⚭⚬

F ROM THIS STUDY a pressing question remains: How shall we live as God's people, given the reality and nature of our spiritual enemy?

All Bible-believing Christians believe Satan and his demons are their enemies. They also believe that in the end God and His people will be victorious and triumphant. Satan and his wicked angels will not win the war; though they certainly seem to be winning some skirmishes and battles, they will be defeated in the end. What evangelical Christians do not agree on is how they are to respond to Satan and the spiritual warfare in which they are engaged.

Many well-intentioned Christian leaders with sincere motives and genuine concern for fellow believers are advocating an offensive response to Satan and the demons. Others with equal fervor and love for God, His Word, and His people believe a defensive response is called for. Which is the more scriptural way? How are we to live as soldiers of the cross? How does God our Captain expect us to make it as pilgrims here, since the devil is the god of this age and the prince of the power of the air, the wicked one who works in the children of disobedience? This is the precise question we want to address in this closing chapter.

First, we need to remind ourselves how fierce our enemy really is. Then we need to remember the great victory our blessed Lord achieved at Calvary.

With those facts in mind, we can better evaluate the offensive approach encouraged by many today. This chapter also discusses more of the defensive approach we should take against the enemy and challenges believers to take advantage of the current interest in angels to refocus people's attention on God.

THE REALITY OF OUR SPIRITUAL ENEMY

Who among Bible believers would question that Satan and his evil hosts are the avowed enemies of God and His people? The existence of Satan is as real and certain as the existence of God. The Bible does not argue for the existence of either; it assumes their existence.

Satan is an evil supernatural being, the believer's subtle adversary who demeans God to people and people to God. He heads a program of spiritual wickedness that encompasses the whole world and every facet of life. He tempts, he lies, he blinds human minds, he distorts, and he is the great accuser of believers. He is the most evil being in the entire universe.

Satan, as we noted earlier, is not all-knowing or all-powerful, and cannot be everywhere at the same time. These characteristics are true only of God. Satan, however, has a host of demons who carry out all his evil desires. They are just as wicked as he is. They too are constantly opposing God and believers, seeking to keep us from everything holy and good. These demons have taken up residence in certain people at times in the past, and they probably still do so in the present. They afflict the saints in every way possible, seeking to lure them away from God and His Word.

THE REALITY OF CHRIST'S VICTORY AT THE CROSS

Satan was defeated and judged at the cross of Christ. Even before our Lord went to the cross, He spoke of His victory over Satan and said that His judgment of him was complete (John 12:31;16:11). The empty tomb provides irrefutable proof that Jesus defeated the devil by His death. That vacant tomb also demonstrates that God the Father accepted God the Son's work.

One of Jesus' last sayings on the cross was, "It is finished." The Greek word He used is *tetelestai* (19:30), which is in the perfect tense and can be translated "It stands finished." All the work He came to do was finished then and remains finished forever. In other words, Christ's victory over Satan, His defeat of him, was certain before Christ ever went to the cross where the work was accomplished.

Though defeated, Satan has not yet been destroyed or put away. The day is coming, however, when he will be cast into the lake of fire (Rev. 20:10). In the meantime, between the time of his defeat at Calvary and his final destination, he and his demons oppose God and afflict the saints on planet earth. Stated another way, the Judge of all the universe has pronounced the verdict on Satan—he was defeated and judged at Golgotha. But Satan is out on bond, as it were, until the appointed day when the punishment stage of that verdict will be carried out.

So we have an enemy who was defeated by our Lord on the cross. In the sovereign plan of God the defeated enemy is free to carry out his evil work on the earth until God's appointed day. At that precise time, not before and not after, His enemy and ours will be forever banished. What a glorious day that will be.

THE CONTEMPORARY OFFENSIVE APPROACH IN SPIRITUAL WARFARE[1]

What does it mean to engage in offensive spiritual warfare? It means the believer is to attack Satan and the demons, to encounter them aggressively. This approach is the opposite of defensive spiritual warfare. Being on the defensive means "resisting or preventing aggression or attack."[2]

The offensive approach is not encouraged in the Bible. As Thomas Ice and Robert Dean wrote, "Man as God's creature has always been in the position of defending himself with God's Word. It appears that for a creature to go on the offensive against Satan is to usurp a divine prerogative reserved for God alone. The creature's posture is trust in God by taking a defensive stance."[3]

The offensive approach encourages people to bind the devil or to demand that he and his demons do certain things. But the Scriptures never tell Christians to do this. The Bible does tell us, however, to resist Satan and to oppose him with the armor of Ephesians 6:10–18. Even our Lord

Himself, when tempted by Satan, did not "bind" him. Instead, Jesus appealed to the Word of God as His defense.

Today believers are told that missionaries must find out which evil spirits are in charge of geographic areas to be evangelized. These must then be driven out before successful evangelization can take place. Such evil spirits are called territorial spirits, and they are said to make it impossible for the gospel to penetrate and the Spirit of God to do His work until they are expelled by someone qualified to do this. Here then is another example of offensive warfare that is nowhere called for in the Bible.

God has willed that Satan be free to roam in this age. He will be bound by God in the future (Rev. 20:1–3), but until that time we are to be prepared for his attacks and to resist him when he comes against us. Scripture does not exhort us to attack Satan aggressively or to search for demons to be cast out.

THE BIBLICAL ANSWER TO "HOW SHALL WE THEN LIVE?"

God has given His people many responsibilities by which to live triumphantly and to carry out the mandates of Scripture. We will survey some of the major ones below. These all involve a defensive mode and are at great variance with the offensive approach encouraged and practiced by many today. Taken together these defensive postures spell out for us how we are to live in this world in view of Satan's power and Christ's provisions for us to be prepared for Satan's certain aggression and attacks.

Responsibilities in Relation to the Word of God

In chapter 8 we dealt with the relation of God's Word to our daily living in a world bombarded by the devil and demons. Here we want only to highlight the indispensability of God's Word to spiritual warfare from a few key passages of Scripture.

Each of these passages states the human responsibility or implies it. Peter said the believer is to "long for the pure milk of the word" (1 Pet. 2:2). Paul exhorted Timothy to study the Scriptures so that he would be able to handle "accurately the word of truth" (2 Tim. 2:15). Jesus told His apostles they were clean as a result of the Word He had given them (John 15:3). The psalmist stressed the same truth (Ps. 119:9).

There is no better way to prepare oneself for Satan's darts and demons than by feeding on God's Word. God does not force His Word on anyone. If we do not believe it and obey it, it will not assist us in spiritual warfare.

Responsibilities in Relation to the World

The child of God is not to love the world or the things in it that distract from Him (1 John 2:15). As noted, the world is every believer's enemy. The anti-God philosophy of the world creeps up on us slyly. Before we know it, we are living by its standards and norms. Believers are to reject and oppose the devil's system.

Responsibilities in Relation to Sin

Each believer is to avoid sin and instead is to "walk in the light," that is, to lead lives of holiness (1 John 1:7). Paul told Timothy to "flee from youthful lusts and pursue righteousness, faith, love and peace" (2 Tim. 2:22). Unfortunately, many Christians try to see how close they can get to sin without actually committing it. The apostle's advice is exactly the opposite.

Responsibilities in Relation to the Holy Spirit

These responsibilities are both positive and negative, as we saw in chapter 8. The believer himself is responsible not to grieve the Spirit (Eph. 4:30), or quench Him (1 Thess. 5:19), but to be filled with (Eph. 5:18) and walk by means of (Gal. 5:16) the Spirit. No one can do these things for us. No amount of commanding demons will get the job done.

Responsibilities in Relation to Christ

God's many commands to His children with respect to Christ are summed up in His word to His own to "abide in Me" (John 15:4). If we do not abide in Him, that is, maintain fellowship with Him, we will not be able to produce spiritual fruit in our lives. Neither will we be able to do battle with Satan unless we "put on" Christ (Rom. 13:14), that is, appropriate Him and His power by faith, and oppose Satan in our Lord's strength.

Responsibilities in Relation to Satan and Temptation

Repeatedly throughout these pages we have referred to the believer's need to resist the devil (James 4:7). No one can do this for us. God has given us the command and the power from the indwelling Holy Spirit to do it. Peter told his Christian readers to do the same thing in their spiritual warfare (1 Pet. 5:9). Paul, in essence, exhorted the Ephesian believers along the same line when he told them to put on the armor of God (Eph. 6:10–18). The various parts of the armor were for defense or protection, not offense.

Responsibilities in Relation to the Angelmania of Our Day

One final obligation rests on God's people in response to the present-day widespread interest in and involvement with angels. It is without doubt the most important of all responsibilities because it is a grand opportunity also. We must use the interest in angels to turn people's attention to the Lord and their need of salvation through faith in Christ.

Jefferey A. Becker stated this response very well. "Given the tenor of our age, the angel emphasis might prove useful in evangelism. If someone is willing to concede the existence of unseen entities, what does that imply about naturalism? Atheism? Who lies behind angels and their activities? Many believers wear a cross to catch people's attention. If you were to see someone wearing an angel, it should catch your attention, causing you to ask, 'What does that pin mean to you?' For if we direct the angel-smitten to Christ, we can truly respond to the current angel craze."[4]

SUMMING IT UP

Obeying God's Word is effective in all parts of the world. There is no special formula for certain areas and no special formula for dealing with certain sins. We are repeatedly called on to live in God's power and to serve Him in His strength. The supernatural enemy, whom every Christian faces, is not to be bound by us or exorcised by us. God in the person of His Son has done all there is to do for Satan's defeat. Our Lord has been victorious and we live and minister in that finished work.

How shall we then live? We should live in the power of the Spirit of God and on the merit of the finished work of Christ. There is no other God-ordained way than the way of the Cross.

Martin Luther, when reflecting on his arrival at the truth of the gospel in contrast to the teaching of Catholicism, said, "The just shall live by faith." He was quoting, of course, Romans 1:17 and Galatians 3:11, where Paul quoted Habakkuk 2:4. (Hebrews 10:38 also quotes that statement from the minor prophet.) When this great truth gripped him, the great Reformer ended his search for how a person could be rightly related to God and how to do battle against Satan.

By God's grace alone, through faith in Christ alone, a condemned sinner enters the family of God. By the same grace of God in the same Christ, redeemed sinners may have victory over the devil and all the demons of hell.

How shall we then live? We should by faith live out the victory already accomplished for us by Christ. This is not faith in the ability to discover the presence and names of territorial demons; not faith in the power to find fetters and bind Satan; not faith that somehow someone will discover why Satan and demons are oppressing or possessing; and not even faith in the ability to cast demons out or denounce them with some special formula or ritual.

In stark contrast to faith in such things, the only way to live the Christian life according to God's Word is by faith in the Son of God, who loved us and gave Himself for us. That is precisely how the apostle Paul lived. He affirmed the same in his testimony to the Galatian Christians (Gal. 2:20).

In each of the New Testament contexts in which Habakkuk 2:4 is quoted (i.e., Rom. 1; Gal. 3; Heb. 10), faith is the means of becoming a child of God and of living as a child of God.

Fellow believer, as you begin each day, remember you are not a victim of Satan. You are a victor in God's army. Live by faith in the One who redeemed you, not in fear of the devil. Live as one who has been delivered, not as one trying to get deliverance. Get on the defensive and off the offensive posture. Keep on the armor of God and do not worry about the size or power of the devil's army. Finally, stay in fellowship with God.

If you are not a believer, you can become a Christian by acknowledging yourself as a sinner, lost and without hope. Place your trust in the Lord Jesus Christ alone. He loved you and gave Himself for you so you need not spend eternity in hell with the devil and his demons.

A Mighty Fortress Is Our God

A mighty fortress is our God, a bulwark never failing;
Our helper He amid the flood of mortal ills prevailing.
For still our ancient foe doth seek to work us woe;
His craft and power are great, and, armed with cruel hate,
On earth is not his equal.

Did we in our own strength confide, our striving would be losing,
Were not the right man on our side, the man of God's own choosing:
Dost ask who that may be? Christ Jesus, it is He;
Lord Sabaoth His name, from age to age the same,
And He must win the battle.

And though this world, with devils filled, should threaten to undo us,
We will not fear, for God hath willed His truth to triumph through us:
The prince of darkness grim, we tremble not for him;
His rage we can endure, for lo, his doom is sure;
One little word shall fell him.

That word above all earthly powers, no thanks to them, abideth;
The Spirit and the gifts are ours through him who with us sideth:
Let goods and kindred go, this mortal life also;
The body they may kill: God's truth abideth still;
His kingdom is forever.[5]

ENDNOTES

CHAPTER 1—TODAY'S ANGELS

1. *Coin & Sportscards Wholesaler* (April/May 1997): 2.
2. *People Weekly*, 23 December 1996, 79–87.
3. Peter Castro, Tom Gliatto, and Samantha Miller, "Angels in America," *People*, 22 December 1997, 79–82, 84.
4. Ibid.
5. *Dallas Morning News*, 31 January 1997.
6. Two examples are Alma Daniel, Timothy Wyllie, and Andrew Ramer, *Ask Your Angel* (New York: Ballantine, 1992); and Sophy Burnham, *A Book of Angels: Reflections on Angels, Past and Present and True Stories of How They Touched Our Lives* (New York: Ballantine, 1990).
7. *Dallas Morning News*, 9 September 1997.
8. Duane Garrett, *Angels and the New Spirituality* (Nashville: Broadman & Holman, 1995), 9.

CHAPTER 2—ANGELS YESTERDAY AND TODAY

1. In this section I have expanded on portions from my *Handbook of Evangelical Theology* (Grand Rapids: Kregel, 1995), chapter 5.
2. In portions of this section I have drawn on Duane A. Garrett's *Angels and the New Spirituality*.

3. See Karl Barth, *Church Dogmatics* (Edinburgh: Clark, 1960), 3.3 for an extended evaluation.

4. Louis Berkhof, *Systematic Theology* (Grand Rapids: Eerdmans, 1968), 141.

5. John Calvin, *Institutes of the Christian Religion*, ed. John T. McNeill (Philadelphia: Westminster, 1967), 1.14.4.

6. Berkhof, *Systematic Theology*, 142.

7. Garrett cites the following: "Thomas rejected the notion of universal matter that the scholar Avicebron had advocated. Many Christian scholars of his day were drawn to the idea but Aquinas saw both the logical errors and dangerous tendencies of the system. See James Collins, *The Thomistic Philosophy of Angels*, Catholic University of American Philosophical Studies 89 (Washington, D.C.: Catholic University of America, 1947), 42–74" (*Angels and the New Spirituality*, 246, n. 4).

8. Ibid., 88–89 (italics his).

9. "The Belgic Confession of Faith," in *Reformed Confessions of the 16th Century*, ed. A. C. Coleridge (Philadelphia: Westminster, 1966), 196.

10. See Calvin, *Institutes of the Christian Religion*, 1.14.3–19. Though not extensive, for the times this was significant.

11. Garrett, *Angels and the New Age Spirituality*, 90.

12. Ibid., 93.

13. For more information on these three men see ibid., 94–101.

14. Ibid., 95.

15. Ibid., 100–101.

16. Tom Minnery, "Unplugging the New Age," *Focus on the Family* (August 1987), 2–3.

17. Philip Lochhaas, "The New Age Movement: Dancing in the Dark," *Lutheran Witness* (April 1987), 80–82.

18. Garrett, *Angels and the New Age Spirituality*, 134.

CHAPTER 3—ANGELS IN THE BIBLE

1. Gustav Davidson, *A Dictionary of Angels* (New York: Free, 1967).

2. *Albuquerque Journal*, 24 November 1996.

3. Davidson, *A Dictionary of Angels*, 340.

4. C. Fred Dickason, *Angels Elect and Evil* (Chicago: Moody, 1975), 32.
5. James Oliver Buswell, *A Systematic Theology of the Christian Religion* (Grand Rapids: Zondervan, 1971), 231–42.

CHAPTER 4—ANGELIC ACTIVITIES IN THE BIBLE

1. Davidson, *A Dictionary of Angels*, 343.
2. See Roy B. Zuck, *Precious in His Sight: Childhood and Children in the Bible* (Grand Rapids: Baker, 1996), 210–11. Others say "their angels" in Matthew 18:10 refers to the spirits of little children who die. However, the Bible gives no support to the common idea that people become angels when they die.
3. Herbert Lockyer, *All the Angels in the Bible* (Peabody, Mass.: Hendrickson, 1996), 68.
4. Davidson, *A Dictionary of Angels*, 342.
5. Burnham, *A Book of Angels*, 133–36.
6. Carolyn Trickey-Bapty, *The Book of Angels* (Ambler, Pa.: Ottenheimer, 1994), 45.
7. Johnson Oatman, Jr., and Jno. R. Sweney, "Holy, Holy, Is What the Angels Sing," *Sing Men, Number Two* (Wheaton, Ill.: Singspiration, 1950), 57. Used by permission.

CHAPTER 5—THE ANGEL CALLED GOD

1. John Peter Lange, *Genesis*, Commentary on the Holy Scriptures, trans. Philip Shaff (Grand Rapids: Zondervan, 1960), 386–91.
2. This has been the historic orthodox position. Some evangelicals have rejected the doctrine of the eternal sonship of Christ and embraced His incarnational sonship. Among the Plymouth Brethren a few held this view and then left the movement. An extensive defense of Christ's eternal sonship is given by George Zeller and Renald Showers, *The Eternal Sonship of Christ* (Neptune, N.J.: Loizeaux Brothers, 1993). The defense of our Lord's eternal sonship given above has been adapted from my *Sin, the Savior, and Salvation* (Grand Rapids: Kregel, 1991).
3. John F. Walvoord, *Jesus Christ Our Lord* (Chicago: Moody, 1969), 42.

4. These evidences indicate the error of Augustine's view, who said the Angel of the Lord is the entire Trinity.

5. Dickason, *Angels Elect and Evil*, 82–83.

CHAPTER 6—THE ANGEL CALLED SATAN

1. For example, Garrett believes Satan is not in view in Ezekiel 28 (*Angels and the New Spirituality*, 39–42). He says "perfect in beauty" is a hyperbole depicting the human ruler of Tyre. "Eden" and "the mountain of God" (28:13–14), Garrett suggests, refer metaphorically to Tyre and its great wealth. He also notes that the references to "trade" (28:16, 18) appropriately apply to Tyre, a seafaring city noted for its extensive trading of many kinds of merchandise (ibid., 40). (Also see George Parsons, "Lucifer before and after His Fall" [Middletown Bible Church, Middletown, Conn., n.d., photocopy].)

    Others say both the king of Tyre and Satan are in view, with Satan being the power behind the human leader (e.g., John MacArthur, *The MacArthur Study Bible* [Nashville: Word, 1997], 1190–91).

2. John A. Martin, "Isaiah," in *The Bible Knowledge Commentary, Old Testament*, ed. John F. Walvoord and Roy B. Zuck (Wheaton, Ill.: Victor, 1985), 1061–62; and Edward J. Young, *The Book of Isaiah*, New International Commentary on the Old Testament (Grand Rapids: Eerdmans, 1965), 440–42.

3. For example, Garrett, *Angels and the New Spirituality*, 36–39.

4. MacArthur, *The MacArthur Study Bible*, 977.

5. The word *Lucifer* (KJV, NKJV) comes from the Hebrew word *hêlēl*, rendered "day star," "star of the morning," or "morning star." *Lucifer* ("light-bearing," from the Latin *lux*, "light") was the Latin name for the planet Venus, the brightest object in the pre-dawn sky. Like this bright object in the sky, which supposedly tries to outshine the sun but whose light is extinguished by it, the person in these verses wanted to be dominant above all others but met a downfall.

6. Some say Lucifer fell during the gap of time presumed to exist between Genesis 1:1 and 1:2. The "gap theory," once popular among evangelicals, conflicts with the grammatical construction of these two verses. Others

say his fall occurred between Genesis 2 and 3, just before Adam and Eve's fall. Preferable is the view that Lucifer became Satan before the creation of the world which is recorded in summary fashion in Genesis 1:1. (See George Zeller, "The Fall of Satan, When Did This Take Place?" [Middletown Bible Church, Middletown, Conn., n.d., photocopy]).

7. *Webster's Third New International Dictionary* (Springfield, Mass.: Merriam-Webster, 1993), 684.

8. Kenneth S. Wuest, *In These Last Days* (Grand Rapids: Eerdmans, 1954), 182.

9. *Webster's Third New International Dictionary*, 2155.

10. Charles C. Ryrie, *Basic Theology* (Wheaton, Ill.: Victor, 1987), 151.

CHAPTER 7—SATAN'S ANGELS

1. Merrill Unger, *Demons in the World Today* (Wheaton, Ill.: Tyndale, 1971), 10.

EXCURSUS—THE "SONS OF GOD" IN GENESIS 6

1. Manfred Kober, "The Sons of God of Genesis 6: Demons, Degenerates, or Despots" (Ankeny, Iowa: Faith Baptist Bible College, n.d.).

2. Allen P. Ross, "Genesis," in *The Bible Knowledge Commentary, Old Testament*, 36.

3. The Nephilim were "people of great size and strength (see Nu[m.]13:31–33). The Hebrew word means 'fallen ones.' In men's eyes they were the 'heroes of old, men of renown,' but in God's eyes they were sinners ('fallen ones') ripe for judgment" (Ronald Youngblood, "Genesis," in *The NIV Study Bible* [Grand Rapids: Zondervan, 1985], 14).

4. Garrett, *Angels and the New Spirituality*, 46.

EXCURSUS—THE SPIRITS IN PRISON IN 1 PETER 3

1. E. Schuyler English, *The Life and Letters of Saint Peter* (New York: "Our Hope," 1945), 209–10.

2. Wayne Grudem, *Systematic Theology* (Downers Grove, Ill.: InterVarsity 1994), 589 (italics his).
3. Kenneth S. Wuest, *First Peter in the Greek New Testament* (Grand Rapids: Eerdmans, 1942), 100.
4. Alan M. Stibbs, *The First Epistle General of Peter* (Grand Rapids: Eerdmans, 1974), 142.
5. Dickason, *Angels Elect and Evil,* 227.
6. J. Ramsey Michaels, *1 Peter,* Word Biblical Commentary (Waco, Tex.: Word, 1988), 205–6.

CHAPTER 8—SATAN, THE SAVIOR, AND THE SAINTS OF GOD

1. For discussion of the opposing view held by most liberals on Genesis 3:15 see the evangelical writers H. C. Leupold (*Exposition of Genesis* [Grand Rapids: Baker, 1942], 163–70) and Jack P. Lewis ("The Woman's Seed [Gen. 3:15]," *Journal of the Evangelical Theological Society* 34 [1991]: 299–319).
2. See Geerhardus Vos, *Biblical Theology* (Grand Rapids: Eerdmans, 1948), 54–55 for further elaboration of this point.
3. For further New Testament authority for understanding Genesis 3:15 as the *protoevangelium* see Derek Kidner, *Genesis,* Tyndale Old Testament Commentaries (Downers Grove, Ill.: InterVarsity, 1967), 70–71.
4. This subject is discussed in most standard works on theology. See especially John F. Walvoord, *Jesus Christ Our Lord* (Chicago: Moody, 1969), 145–52, and John A. Witmer, *Immanuel—"God with Us"* (Nashville: Word, 1998).
5. See my *Handbook of Evangelical Theology,* 250–62 for more discussion on these enemies of Christians.
6. Fritz Rienecker, *A Linguistic Key to the Greek New Testament,* ed. Cleon L. Rogers, Jr. (Grand Rapids: Zondervan, 1980), 457.
7. Some say each believer has only a new nature (e.g., David C. Needham, *Birthright* [Portland, Oreg.: Multnomah, 1979]). But this view has two serious weaknesses. It must redefine sin for the believer, and it fails to distinguish the believer's position before God from his practice on earth. MacArthur and other "lordship salva-

tion" proponents also hold this view. He wrote, "I believe it is a serious misunderstanding to think of the believer as having both an old and new nature. Believers do not have dual personalities . . . there is no such thing as an old nature in the believer" (*Freedom from Sin— Romans 6–7* [Chicago: Moody, 1987], 31–32). For a further refutation of this view, see Lewis Sperry Chafer, *He That Is Spiritual* (1918; reprint, Grand Rapids: Zondervan, 1967), and Renald E. Showers, *The New Nature* (Neptune, N.J.: Loizeaux Brothers, 1986).

8. Robert T. Ketcham explains this concept in Ephesians 6 in *God's Provisions for Normal Christian Living* (Chicago: Moody, 1963).

CHAPTER 9—GOD'S SON AND GOD'S ANGELS

1. The most extensive discussion of this subject is to be found in George W. Zeller and Renald E. Showers, *The Eternal Sonship of Christ* (Neptune, N.J.: Loizeaux Brothers, 1993).
2. Lockyer, *All the Angels in the Bible*, 99–100.
3. Observe the meaning and significance of this in J. A. Seiss, *The Apocalypse* (Grand Rapids: Zondervan, 1957), 521, and John F. Walvoord, *The Revelation of Jesus Christ* (Chicago: Moody, 1967), 35, 336–40.
4. Garrett, *Angels and the New Spirituality,* 56–57.

CHAPTER 10—DEMON POSSESSION IN THE NEW TESTAMENT

1. Alex Konya has an excellent summary of the meaning and uses of these words and phrases in *Demons: A Biblically Based Perspective* (Schaumburg, Ill.: Regular Baptist, 1990), 20–23.
2. Sydney H. T. Page has a helpful discussion of this issue in *Powers of Evil* (Grand Rapids: Baker, 1995), 138.
3. Konya, *Demons: A Biblically Based Perspective*, 22.
4. Unger, *Demons in the World Today*, 113.
5. For various views of this passage see Paige Patterson, *The Troubled Triumphant Church* (Nashville: Nelson, 1983), 85–90.
6. Ryrie, *Basic Theology*, 167.
7. The word *occult* comes from the Latin *occultus* meaning "something

hidden, secret, or mysterious." The word describes things that seem to be beyond people's natural experiences.

8. Konya, *Demons: A Biblically Based Perspective*, 28–31.
9. Ibid., 30–31.

CHAPTER 11—DEMON EXORCISM IN THE NEW TESTAMENT

1. John J. Davis, *Demons, Exorcism and the Evangelical* (Winona Lake, Ind.: BMH, 1977), 9.
2. Peter Toon, "Exorcism," in *The New International Dictionary of the Christian Church*, ed. J. D. Douglas (Grand Rapids: Zondervan, 1974), 365.
3. These four are given thorough treatment by Page in *Powers of Evil*, 137–68.
4. For a discussion of the problem of exactly where this miracle took place see Bruce M. Metzger, *A Textual Commentary on the Greek New Testament* (London: United Bible Societies, 1971), 23, and C. H. Kraeling, ed., *Gerasa: City of Decapolis* (New Haven, Conn.: American Schools of Oriental Research, 1938).
5. Some New Testament scholars believe the two accounts by Matthew (9:32–34 and 12:22–24) are doublets. Others view them as two separate exorcisms. For the doublets view see Robert Gundry, *Matthew: A Commentary on His Literary and Theological Art* (Grand Rapids: Eerdmans, 1982), 179, 231. For the two-separate-miracles view see W. M. Alexander, *Demonic Possession in the New Testament* (Edinburgh: Clark, 1902).
6. Konya, *Demons: A Biblically Based Perspective*, 41.
7. Ibid., 43–44.
8. George Eldon Ladd, *Jesus and the Kingdom: The Eschatology of Biblical Realism* (New York: Harper & Row, 1964), 149.
9. *Chicago Tribune*, August 28, 1996, cited by David M. Gorver, "Dealing with the Devil," *Baptist Bulletin* (April 1997): 13.
10. Konya, *Demons: A Biblically Based Perspective*, 81.
11. For a discussion of the temporary nature of the sign gifts, see my *Speaking in Tongues and Divine Healing*, 2d ed. (Schaumburg, Ill.: Regular Baptist, 1978).

CHAPTER 12:—SPIRITUAL WARFARE—MAN'S WAY AND GOD'S

1. David Powlison, *Power Encounters: Reclaiming Spiritual Warfare* (Grand Rapids: Baker, 1995), 49–61. Powlison presents an excellent discussion of spiritual warfare in the Old and New Testaments.
2. C. Peter Wagner, *Confronting the Powers* (Ventura, Calif.: Regal, 1996).
3. Ibid., 30.
4. John F. Hart critiques Wagner's approach thoroughly and fairly ("The Gospel and Spiritual Warfare," review of *Confronting the Powers*, by Peter Wagner, *Journal of the Grace Evangelical Society* 10 [Spring 1997]: 29–39).
5. Adapted from Terry C. Hulbert, "Spiritual Warfare" (paper presented at the annual meeting of The Evangelical Alliance Mission, May 1992, 2–3).
6. C. Peter Wagner, "Territorial Spirits," in *Wrestling with Dark Angels* (Ventura, Calif.: Regal, 1990), 77.
7. Ibid., 76.
8. See Clinton E. Arnold, *Powers of Darkness: Principalities and Powers in Paul's Letters* (Downers Grove, Ill.: InterVarsity, 1992).
9. Ed Murphy, "We Are at War," in *Wrestling with Dark Angels*, ed. C. Peter Wagner and F. Douglas Pennoyer (Ventura, Calif.: Regal, 1990), 51, 58 (italics his).
10. Ibid., 65 (italics his).
11. Louis A. Barbieri, "Matthew," in *The Bible Knowledge Commentary, New Testament*, ed. John F. Walvoord and Roy B. Zuck (Wheaton, Ill.: Victor, 1983), 46.
12. Powlison, *Power Encounters: Reclaiming Spiritual Warfare*, 28.

CHAPTER 13—COMMONLY ASKED QUESTIONS ABOUT ANGELS AND DEMONS

1. Dickason, *Angels Elect and Evil*, 32.
2. Buswell, *A Systematic Theology of the Christian Religion*, 235–36.

3. Trickey-Bapty, *The Book of Angels*, 30.

4. Garrett, *Angels and the New Spirituality*, 116–17.

5. Trickey-Bapty, *The Book of Angels*, 24.

6. Charles C. Ryrie, *The Ryrie Study Bible* (Chicago: Moody, 1978), 471.

7. Kenneth Boa and William Proctor, *The Return of the Star of Bethlehem* (Garden City, N.Y.: Doubleday, 1980), 123. Also see Zuck, *Precious in His Sight,* 185–87.

8. James Arthur Woychuck, "The Biblical Relationship between Stars and Angels" (Th.M. thesis, Dallas Theological Seminary, 1996).

9. For further defense of this view see Augustus Seiss, *The Apocalypse: Lectures on the Book of Revelation* (Grand Rapids: Zondervan, n.d.), 51–52. For the opposing view see Gerhard Friedrich Kittel, "*angellos*," in *Theological Dictionary of the New Testament*, ed. Gerhard Friedrich Kittel, trans. Geoffrey W. Bromiley (Grand Rapids: Eerdmans, 1967), 1:186–87.

10. Ryrie, *The Ryrie Study Bible.*

CHAPTER 14—HOW SHALL WE THEN LIVE?

1. In chapter 12 we examined some of these issues.

2. *Webster's New International Dictionary*, 591.

3. Thomas Ice and Robert Dean, *Overrun by Demons: The Church's New Preoccupation with the Demonic* (Eugene, Oreg.: Harvest, 1990), 178.

4. Jefferey A. Becker, "How to Respond to the Current Angel Craze," *Baptist Bulletin* (September, 1997):16.

5. Martin Luther, "A Mighty Fortress Is Our God," in *Hymns for the Living Church* (Carol Stream, Ill.: Hope, 1974), 11.

BIBLIOGRAPHY

Anders, Max. *What You Need to Know about Spiritual Warfare in Twelve Lessons*. Nashville: Thomas Nelson Publishers, 1997.

Arnold, Clinton E. *Powers of Darkness: Principalities and Powers in Paul's Letters*. Downers Grove, Ill.: InterVarsity Press, 1992.

_____. *Three Crucial Questions about Spiritual Warfare*. Grand Rapids: Baker Book House, 1997.

Bubeck, Mark I. *Overcoming the Adversary*. Chicago: Moody Press, 1984.

Bufford, Rodger K. *Counseling and the Demonic*. Dallas: Word Books, 1988.

Davidson, Gustav. *A Dictionary of Angels*. New York: Free Press, 1967.

Davis, John J. *Demons, Exorcism and the Evangelical*. Winona Lake, Ind.: BMH Books, 1977.

Dickason, C. Fred. *Angels Elect and Evil*. Chicago: Moody Press, 1975.

Garrett, Duane A. *Angels and the New Spirituality*. Nashville: Broadman & Holman Publishers, 1995.

Graham, Billy. *Angels: God's Secret Agents*. Garden City, N.Y.: Doubleday & Co., 1975.

Ice, Thomas, and Robert Dean. *Overrun by Demons: The Church's New Preoccupation with the Demonic*. Eugene, Oreg.: Harvest House, 1990.

James, Peter. *Spirit Wars*. Mukilteo, Wash.: Wine Press Publishing Co., 1997.

Jeremiah, David. *What the Bible Says about Angels*. Sisters, Oreg.: Multnomah Press, 1996.

Konya, Alex. *Demons: A Biblically Based Perspective*. Schaumburg, Ill.: Regular Baptist Press, 1990.

Lockyer, Herbert. *All the Angels in the Bible*. Peabody, Mass.: Hendrickson Publishers, 1996.

————. *Satan, His Person and Power*. Waco, Tex.: Word Books, 1980.

Montgomery, John W., ed. *Demon Possession*. Minneapolis: Bethany Fellowship Publishers, 1976.

Page, Sydney H. T. *Powers of Evil*. Grand Rapids: Baker Book House, 1995.

Powlison, David. *Power Encounters: Reclaiming Spiritual Warfare*. Grand Rapids: Baker Book House, 1995.

Swindoll, Charles R. *Demonism: How to Win against the Devil*. Portland, Oreg.: Multnomah Press, 1981.

Unger, Merrill F. *Demons in the World Today*. Wheaton, Ill.: Tyndale House Publishers, 1971.

————. *What Demons Can Do to Saints*. Chicago: Moody Press, 1991.

Wagner, C. Peter, and Douglas F. Pennoyer, eds. *Wrestling with Dark Angels*. Ventura, Calif.: Regal Books, 1990.

SCRIPTURE INDEX

Genesis

1	141
1:26	34
1:28	167
1:31	66
2:15/16–17	77
3	33, 73, 108
3:1	77
3:1–3	78
3:1–6	74
3:4/5	78
3:7–9	74
3:14	106
3:15	78, 106, 107
3:24	30, 69
6	90, 95
6:1–2	96
6:1–4	95, 96, 101
6:1–6	94
6:2	89, 94, 95, 96, 97
6:4	95
11:4	95
12:1–3	56
14:18–19	72
16:1–7	56

16:7	55
16:8/10–12	56
16:13	56, 62
18:1–2	170
19	38
19:1	170
21:17	62
22:12	57
22:15–16	62
22:16–17	57
24:3	139
27	57
28:10–12/17	39
31:11	39, 57, 62
31:13	39
31:13	57
32:1–2	40
32:2	28
32:24/27–28	57
32:29–30	58
48:15–16	62

Exodus

3:2/4–5/6/7–10	58

3:14	55
13:9	62
13:21	60
14:19	60, 62
21:6	95
22:8–9/28	95
23:20	40, 43
23:23	40
25:17–22	31
32:34	40
33:2	40
33:14	55

Leviticus

17:7	86, 92

Numbers

15:32–36	164
22:22–27	60
22:31	54

Deuteronomy

18:10–11	175
32	86

32:17	87, 92, 135

Joshua
5:14	55

Judges
2:1–2/3/4–5	59
5:20	171
6:1–24	59
9:23	92
13:2–5/8/10–12/	
20/22	60

1 Samuel
16:1	122, 132
16:14	92, 131
17:12	122
28:3/4/7/11/12	175
28:16–17	150
28:19	176

2 Samuel
14:20	27
24:16–17	60

1 Kings
19:3–4/5–8	43
19:5	8, 47
22:19	25

2 Kings
1:2	74
19:35	60

1 Chronicles
21:1	73

Job
1:6	26, 28, 70, 96
1:6–9	73
1:9	70
1:12	73
2:1	26, 28, 70, 96
2:1–4/6–7	73

2:7	70
15:15	171
25:5	171
38:4	26
38:7	26, 28, 96, 171

Psalms
40:8	115
48:2	72
68:4	72
68:17	25
68:17–18	124
82:6	95
89:6	28
91:11/12–13	47
103:1	45
103:20	27, 45
103:20–21	25, 28
104:3	72
104:4	28, 89
106:36–37	135
106:37	87
119:9	183
119:105/125/131	115
148:2	25
148:3	171
148:5	25

Proverbs
24:19	81

Ecclesiastes
1:9	9

Isaiah
2:2–3	72
6	168
6:1–6	32
6:1–7	45
6:2	168
6:2–6	31
6:3	31, 32, 45
6:6–7	45
9:6	61

14:1–3	71
14:1–11	71
14:3–21	72
14:4	72
14:4–19	71
14:12	71, 73
14:12–15	71
14:12–17	67, 72
14:12–19	67, 70, 71
14:13	72
14:13–14	33, 72, 78, 108
14:14	72
14:15	71, 73
14:15–19	71
14:16–17	73
14:16–20	71
19:1	72
36—37	71
37:36	60
42:6	152

Jeremiah
15:16	115
31:31–40	145

Ezekiel
1	167
1—24	68
1:4–24	31
1:5	69
1:5–6	31
1:11	168
10	45
10:5/9	69
10:15–20	31
25—32	68
28:2	69
28:2–10	69, 70
28:9	69
28:11–19	67, 68, 70
28:12	69
28:12–13	69
28:13	69

28:14	30, 69, 72	2:2/8	122	14:30	75
28:15	69, 107	2:13	48, 122	15:21–28	142
28:15–18	70	2:19–20	48, 178	15:22	134, 142
28:16	30, 69, 72	3:17	108	15:22–28	87
33—39	69	4:1	76, 107	15:26	143
36:24–38	145	4:1–10	122	15:28	148
37:21–28	145	4:1–11	107, 115	16:11	75
40—48	69	4:3	76, 108	16:19	157
		4:5–6/9	108	16:27	44
Daniel		4:10–11	84	17:14–18	89
3:16–18/25	42	4:11	107, 122	17:14–21	143
3:28	27	4:24	93, 129, 144	17:15	87
4:13/17/23	28	5:12–13	138	17:15–18	92
6:22	27, 43, 47	5:28	111	17:16	145
7:10	25	6:25/26–31	81	18:10	47
7:15–27	125	7:21–23	147	18:18	157
8	29	8:16	89, 90, 144	22:23–24	26
8:13–26	125	8:28	134	22:30	26, 166, 167
8:15–22	29	8:28–34	141	24:29–31	29
8:20/21	29	9:2	134	24:37–39	97
9:20–27	125	9:32–34	144	25:31	125
9:21	29, 168	9:33	92	25:41	87, 89, 117
10:13/20	156	9:34	74	26:36–38/53	123
10:28	29	10:1	87, 133,	26:63	139
12:1	30		145, 148,	28:2	27, 32
			156, 174	28:4/6	123
Hosea		10:6	143	28:20	113
12:3–4	58	10:8	157, 174		
		10:25	74	**Mark**	
Habakkuk		10:27	146	1:3	172
2:4	185	12:22	87, 92, 134,	1:12–13	107
			146	1:23	130, 134
Zechariah		12:22–24	144	1:23–28	140
1:8–17	60	12:24	74, 87, 89, 141,	1:24	140, 141
1:12–13	62		144, 146	1:25	141
3:1–2	62, 73	12:25–26	74	1:26	134
3:1–10	60	12:27	139	1:27	90
5:9	167	12:28	87	1:32/34	144
		12:29	157	1:39	140
Malachi		12:31	74, 75	3:22	144
3:1	55	13:24–30	44	3:30	130
		13:37–42	133	5:1–20	88, 92, 141
Matthew		13:37–43	44	5:2	130, 141
1:20/24–25	121	13:49–50	126	5:3–4	142

5:5	134	4:36	128	1:14	25, 107
5:7/9/10/11–12	142	4:41	144	1:18	61
5:15/18	130	6:18	134	1:48	107
6:13	145	7:21	93, 129	3:16	61
7:24–30	142	7:24	172	5:14	134
8:38	125	7:33	130	5:18	61
9:14–29	143, 145	8:2	144	7:20	130
9:17	89, 134	8:26–39	141	10:21	61
9:17–18	143	8:27	130, 134	10:30–48	61
9:18–20	134	8:28	142	12:31	81, 108,
9:21–22	143	8:36	130		156, 180
9:25	90	9:1	145	14:16–17	113
9:25–26	143	9:37–43	143	14:23	107
9:38	139, 147	9:40	145	14:26	114
9:39/40	147	9:42	148	14:30	108, 156
13:32	32	9:49–50	139	15:3/4	183
16:5–6	36	9:52	172	15:10	115
16:9	144	10	71	15:18–20	112
16:17	145	10:1	146, 148	16:1–3	112
		10:9	146	16:11	108, 109,
Luke		10:17	71, 90, 146,		156, 180
1:5	119		148, 156	16:13	114
1:7	120	10:18	71, 146	17:14	112
1:8–9	43	10:20	90	17:15	76
1:11	120	11:14–15/19	144	19:30	109, 180
1:11–12	29	11:24	133	20:1–9	124
1:11–13	43	12:19	111	20:5	42
1:12–13	xii	13:11–16	131, 132	20:12	124
1:13/15/17	120	13:32	144	20:28–31	61
1:19	29, 32	15:10	42		
1:20	120	17:26–29	97		
1:27–28	44	18:	10		
1:28	120	20:36	167	*Acts*	
1:30–31	44	22:3	89	1:9/10–11	124
1:30–34	29	22:43	118, 123	1:15–26	145
1:31/32/34	120	22:44/47–50	123	5:3	131, 132
1:35/38	22, 120	24:4	26	5:12	148
2:6-7/9/11	121	24:12	42	5:12–16	145
2:13	25, 27, 122	24:50–51	124	5:16	134, 135
4:1–12	67			5:17–18	40
4:1–13	107	*John*		5:17–24	43
4:5	104	1:1	25	5:21–42	40
4:33–37	140	1:1–3	165	6:6	145
4:34	140, 141	1:3	24, 107	7:53	125

8:6–7   148
8:7   130, 146
8:26   40
10   158
10:3   38
10:7   39
10:30   26
10:38   148
12:1–23   41
12:3–12   43
12:7–9   162
12:23   27
16:16   135
16:18   145
17:11   115
19:8–20   135
19:11–12   135, 148
19:13   139, 147
19:13–16   91, 135
19:14–16   139
19:19   136
23:8   26
27:22–24   43

Romans
1   185
1:16   34, 157
1:17   185
1:21–32   86
5:12   33, 77
6:12   158
7   111
7:18   80, 111
8:29   34
8:32   61
8:38   31
12:3   111
13:14   113, 159, 184

1 Corinthians
4:9   41
5:5   131, 132
6:3   33
6:19   113

6:19–20   111
10:20   92
10:20–21   135
11:10   41
12:9   148
14:22   148
15:35–45   171
15:40   166

2 Corinthians
2:11   78, 79, 110, 152
4:2–5   75
4:4   75, 86, 156
5:20   176
5:21   107
6:15–16   133
11:3   67, 74
11:4   133
11:14   26, 64, 65,
               79, 131, 132
12:2   11, 32
12:4   11
12:7   92, 131, 132, 133
12:12   145

Galatians
1:8   32
2:20   185
3   185
3:11   185
3:16   107
3:19   125
4:4   61
5:16   80, 114, 183
5:17   111

Ephesians
1:21   31, 42
2:2   75, 156
3:10   24, 27, 31, 42
4:22–25   34, 164
4:27   117, 160
4:30   114, 183
5:18   80, 114, 132, 183

5:25–26   115
6   161, 173
6:10–11   153
6:10–17   93
6:10–18   181, 184
6:10–20   159
6:11   82, 113, 117
6:11–18   110
6:12   24, 31, 89,
       91, 97, 113, 133
6:13   113, 159, 161
6:14   158
6:14–17 113, 159, 161
6:17   115
6:18   113, 159, 161

Philippians
3:21   107

Colossians
1:14   93
1:15   107
1:15–16   24
1:16   25, 31
1:16–17   61, 165
1:17   107
2:10   24, 31
2:14   101
2:15   24, 31, 101, 107
2:18   33, 46, 165
3:9–10   34, 164

1 Thessalonians
2:18   110, 156
3:5   76
4:16   29, 125
5:19   114, 183

2 Thessalonians
2:4   71

1 Timothy
4:1–3   90, 91
5:21   27, 30, 42

6:16	26	4:7–10	159, 160	*Revelation*	
		4:8	160	1:1	125
2 Timothy				2-3	172
2:15/22	115, 183	*1 Peter*		3:5	30
3:15/16–17	115	1:12	27, 34, 42	4:8	45
		1:23	115	5:1/2/3–7	124
Hebrews		2:2	115, 182	5:6	167
1–2	126, 127	3	102	5:11	32, 125
1:1–3	126	3:18	101	5:11–12	25
1:2	61, 107, 165	3:18–20	99, 101	5:12	46
1:4–14	126	3:19	100, 101	7:1	44
1:5	45	3:22	101	7:11	32
1:6	25, 127	5:6	79	8—9	30, 44
1:7	38, 127	5:7	79, 81, 161	8:3	44
1:8–9	127	5:8	74, 79, 82,	9:1–11	91
1:14	28, 38, 47,		110, 117, 153	9:11	30, 91
	127, 169	5:8–9	159, 160	9:13	89
2:2	125	5:9	79, 161, 184	9:13–19	91
2:2–3	127			10:1	26
2:3–4	148	*2 Peter*		12:3–4	76
2:5–7	127	1:3	80	12:4	88-89
2:5–18	126	1:19	171	12:7	30, 76
2:9	32, 33	2:1–2	91	12:7–13	70
3:1–6	126	2:4	89, 97, 100, 101	12:9	67, 76, 77,
4:2–10	126	2:4–5	96, 101		79, 146
4:12	115	2:10/13–14/18	91	12:10	70
4:14	32			12:13/16–17	76
4:14—5:10	126	*1 John*		13:1–4	76
6:1	126	1:1–3	61	14:6	168
7:1–28	126	1:5	93	14:14–16	72
8:1–13	126	1:7	183	14:18	30, 44
9:1—10:18	126	2:13–14	76	15—16	45
10	185	2:15	81, 112, 158, 183	16	30
10:38	185	2:16	81	16:1	28
12:22	25	3:12	76	16:5	30
13:5	113, 116	4:1–4	91, 92	16:13	76
		4:4	116	16:13–16	92
James		4:10/14	61	16:14	91
1:13/14–15	173	5:18–19	76	18:1	26
1:18/23–24	115			19:1–6	29
2:19	90	*Jude*		19:10	46
2:25	28, 172	6	100, 101	20:1–2	30
4	161	6-7	96, 97	20:1–3	70, 157,
4:7	117, 149, 153, 158,	9	29, 30, 116		161, 182
	160, 161, 184	13	171	20:2	67, 76

20:3	73	20:10	70, 73, 109, 117, 181	22:9	33, 46
20:7–10	161			22:16	125, 171
20:8/9	117	22:8–9	165		

SUBJECT INDEX

—∞∞∞—

—A—

A Book of Angels, 17–18
Abednego, 42
Abimilech, 92
Abraham, 56, 170
Adam and Eve
    and Satan, 77–78
Ananias, 132
Anderson, Joan Webster, 17
Angel collectibles, 4–6
Angel (gold coin), 2
Angel Letters, 168
Angel, meaning of word, 37
Angel Museum (Beloit, WI), 4
Angel of the abyss, 30
Angel of the Lord, 55–63
    as preincarnate Christ, 60–63
    ministries listed, 63
    titles, 55
Angel of the waters, 30
Angelmania. *See* Angelphilia
Angelphilia, vs. Bible view, 5, 48–52,
    163, 184
Angels
    Bible views, 23–24, 30, 37–52, 172

characteristics, 26–28, 164–65, 167,
    168, 170–71
cherubim, 30–31
Christ and, 33, 38, 48, 51
classes of, 10
contact with, 38–39, 49–50, 168,
    169–70
creation of, 24–26
early church ideas, 9–11
fall of, 174–75
gender, 167
Gnostic views, 10
guardian, 46–48, 168–69
heaven and, 31–33
humans and, 33–34
in God's image, 164
liberalism on, 14
lower than Jesus Christ, 126–27
Middle Ages views, 11–12
ministry of, 50–51, 163–64
modern teachings, 14–16
names of, 28–31
New Age teachings, 17–20
numbers of, 25, 26

popular culture, ix–x, 1–6, 166
praying to, 46, 166
Reformation views, 12–13
relationship with Christ, 119–28
salvation and, 33, 42, 166, 176
seraphim, 31
stars and, 171–72
worship of, 9, 165–66.
See also Demons; Gabriel; Michael
Angels and the New Spirituality (book), 5
Angels: God's Secret Agents, 14
"Angels in Fort Worth" (sculpture), 5
Angels: Ministers of Grace (book), 16
Angels of Mercy (book), 18
Angels on Earth (magazine), 1
"Angels Watching Over Me" (song), ix
Angels within Us, The (book), 18
Apocrypha, 23
Aquinas, Thomas, 11–12, 19, 168
Armageddon, 92
Ask Your Angels (book), 17, 18–19

—B—

Balaam's donkey, 60
Barna, George, 154
Barth, Karl, 15–16
Becker, Jefferey A., 184
Beelzebul, 74
Belgic Confession, on angels, 12
Bible, angels in, 5–6, 23–34
    as protection, 115–16
    on heavens 32–33
    vs. angelphilia, 48–52
Blatty, William, 139
Book of Mormon, 23
Burnham, Sophy, 17, 168

—C—

Cabala, on angels, 23, 25
Calvin, John, 12–13, 19
    on classes of angels, 10–11
Cassels, Louis, 14

Casting out demons. *See* Exorcism
Celestial Hierarchy, 10
Cherubim, 30–31, 69
Christ. *See* Jesus Christ
Christian life, Satan and, 109–16
Christian teachings on angels
    early church, 9–11
    Middle Ages, 11–12
    modern, 14–16.
    See also Angels, Bible views
Clark, Marcia, 3
Contacting angels, 169–70
Cornelius, 38–39

—D—

Daniel (prophet), 28–30, 42–43, 47
Daniel, Alma, 17
Dante, 13
Darius, 42–43, 47
Davidson, Gustav, 23, 28
Davis, John, 139
Dead Sea Scrolls, 23
Dean, Robert, 181
Deliverance ministries, 153, 156–59, 174, 181–82
    binding Satan, 156–58
Demon influence, 131, 173–74
Demon possession, 129–36
    believers and, 131–33
    cause, 134–36
    Christians and, 173–74
    occult and, 135–36
Demons, 77, 85–98, 163–64
    activities, 92–93, 17–73
    characteristics, 85–86, 88, 90–92, 172
    exorcism, 156, 157
    Genesis, 6, 94–98
    New Testament, 87–88
    Old Testament, 86–87
    origin, 88–89
    Tribulation, 91–92
    what they know, 164–65.

See also Demon possession;
Exorcism; Satan
Devil. *See* Satan
Devils. *See* Demons
Dickason, C. Fred, 63, 164
Dictionary of Angels (book), 23, 28
Dionysius the Areopagite, 10
Divine Comedy, 13
Dixon, Jeanne, 14
Dragon, Satan as, 76
Dukes, Juliana, 24
Duns Scotus, 11

—E—

Early church, idea of angels, 9–11
Eleven, the, 148. *See also* Exorcism
Elijah, 43, 47
Elizabeth, 119–20
English, E. Schuyler, 99–100
Evil spirit, in Old Testament, 92
Evil spirits. *See* Demons; Satan
Exorcism, 139–49
    by apostles, 145–46
    by Jesus, 140–45
    by non–Christians, 146
    New Testament word use, 139
    today, 147–49, 174
Exorcist, The (book/film), 139
Ezekiel, 68–70

—F—

Fall of man, 77–78
Fallen angels. *See* Demons
Faust, 13
Flesh, the, 111
Flood, demons and, 96–97
Four living creatures, 45

—G—

Gabriel, 28–29, 119–21, 168
Garrett, Duane, 5, 11–12, 16, 96
Gideon, 59
Gift of Prophecy, A, 14

Gnostics, on angels, 10
God, angels and, 45–46
"God of this world," Satan as, 75
Graham, Billy, 14
Grant, Amy, ix
Guardian angels, 168–69
    of humans, 46–48
    of planets, 46
    Reformation view, 12
Guardians of Hope, 18
Guideposts (magazine), on angels, 1, 2–3
Guiley, Rosemary Ellen, 18

—H—

Hagar, 56, 62
Healing, and casting out demons, 148
Heaven, 31–33
Herod Agrippa, 40–41
Holy Spirit, 113–14, 183
Hosts of angels, 28
Hulburt, Terry C., 154–55

—I—

Ice, Thomas, 181
Idol worship
    demons and, 86–87, 92
    possession and, 135–37
Isaac, 19, 56–57, 170
Isaiah, 70–73
Ishmael, 56
Islam on angels, 164
Israelites, angel and, 58–59, 60

—J—

Jacob, 39–40, 57–58
Jennings, Peter, 4
Jesus Christ, 183–84
    angels and, 33, 38, 48, 51, 119–28
    as Angel of the Lord, 55–63
    eternal existence, 119
    exorcism, 140–45
    "king of angels" title, 165
    overcoming Satan, 12–16

...cability, 108–9
 return, 125–26
 Satan's hostility, 105–9
 victorious over Satan, 180–81
John the Baptist, 119–20
John XXIII, 166
Joseph, 48, 121, 122
Judaism on angels, 32, 164
Judgment, angels and, 30, 44–45

—K—

Kober, Manfred, 95
Konya, Alex, 130, 144, 148
Koran, 23

—L—

Lakey, Andy, 3–4
Lochhaas, Philip, 17
Lockyer, Herbert, 48
Lot, 38
Lucifer. See Satan
Lucky angel coin, 2
Luther, Martin, 185

—M—

MacGregor, Geddes, 16
Manoah and wife, 59–60
Mary, mother of Jesus, 48, 120–21
Medium of Endor, 175–76
Mephistopheles, 13
Meshach, 42
Michael, 9, 28, 29–30, 116
 in New Age sources, 18
 Israel and, 30
Middle Ages, angel beliefs in, 11–12
Milton, John, 12–13, 19
Ministering spirits, 38
Minnery, Tom, 16–17
Modern period, interest in angels, 19–20
Montgomery, Ruth, 14
Moroni (angel), 18
Moses, 30, 40, 58, 86–87

Murphy, Ed, 156

—N—

Nebuchadnezzar, 42
Nephilim, 94, 95–98, 100
New Age teachings, 16–17
 key teachings listed, 17
 on angels, 5, 17–20
 on self-actualization, 18

—O—

Occult beliefs
 on angels, 32
 popularity, 14
 possession and, 135–36
Origen, 168

—PQ—

Paradise Lost, 13
Paul, apostle, 41–42, 43, 110
People magazine, angel stories, 3–4
Peter, apostle, 38–39, 40–41, 42, 43, 110
Philip, evangelist, 40, 145–46
Pius XI, 166
Powlison, David, 152, 158
Prayer, to angels, 46, 166
Price, John Randolph, 18
"Prince," Satan as, 74–75
Pseudepigrapha, 23
Pseudo-Dionysius, 10
Publishers Clearing House, 4–5
Quran. See Koran

—R—

Ramer, Andrew, 17
Rationalism, angels and, 14
Reagan, Ronald, 4
Reformation teaching, on angels, 12–13
Revelation, angels in, 30, 172
Ross, Allen, 95
Ruler, Satan as, 74–75
Ryrie, Charles, 81, 133, 175–76

—S—

Saints, victory over Satan, 112–16
Samson, 59–60
Samuel, ghost of, 175–76
Sarah, 56, 170
Satan, 65–84, 110–11, 184
  as angel of light, 65
  as cherub, 30, 69
  as creature, 9, 66
  avoiding his snares, 78–82, 182–86
  Bible view, 66–67
  binding, 156–58
  characteristics, 67, 110, 116–17
  Christians and, 179–87
  conflict with Jesus, 105–9
  defeat, 30, 67–73, 106–9, 116–17,
    180–81
  existence doubted, 172
  humans and, 77–78, 109–16
  meaning of word, 73
  names in Bible, 73–77
  offensive response to, 179, 181–82.
  See also Demons; Exorcism
Saul, 175–76
Sceva's sons, 147
Schaeffer, Francis, x
Scriptures. See Bible
Seraphim, 31, 45
Serpent, as Satan, 67, 74, 77–78.
  See also Satan
Seventy, casting out demons, 71, 90,
  146, 174
Shadrach, 42
Shepherds at Jesus' birth, 121–22
Simpson, Nicole Brown, 3
Sin, 183
  Satan and, 77–78, 79–80
"Sons of God" in Genesis, 94–98
Spirits, in New Testament, 101
"Spirits in prison," 99–102
Spiritual warfare, 151–62, 181–82
  biblical, 158–61
  cause, 151

contemporary types, 153–55
New Testament, 152–53
Old Testament, 152
reasons for increase, 153–55
Stars, angels and, 171–72
Stibbs, Alan M., 100
Summa theologica, on angels, 11–12
Superstition, about angels, 1–3
Swedenborg, Emanuel, 15

—T—

Tartarus, 100–102
Taylor, Terry Lynn, 18
Temptation
  of believers, 184
  of Jesus, 105, 107–9
Tempter, Satan as, 76
Territorial spirits, 155–56, 182
"Third wave" idea, 18
Timothy, 42
Toon, Peter, 139
Touched by an Angel (TV program), ix
Tribulation, 30

—UV—

Unclean spirits, 87
Unger, Merrill F., 86, 131

—W—

Wagner, C. Peter, 155
Walvoord, John F., 62
Watchers, 28
Where Angels Walk (book), 17
Winfrey, Oprah, 4
Witch of Endor. See Medium of Endor
Word of God, 115–16, 184–86
  spiritual warfare and, 182–83.
  See also Bible, angels in
Work, Satan and, 81–82
World, the, 111–12
  Satan and, 81, 183
Worry, Satan and, 80–81
Woychuck, James, 171–72

V., 76, 100
.othy, 17

—XYZ—
Zacharias, 43–44, 119–20

Zechariah, 60, 62
Zodiac, angel beliefs, 49
Zohar, 23